# Just Wives?

# Just Wives?
## Stories of Power and Survival in the Old Testament and Today

*Katharine Doob Sakenfeld*

Westminster John Knox Press
LOUISVILLE • LONDON

Scripture quotations, unless otherwise indicated, are from the New Revised Standard Version of the Bible, copyright © 1989 by the Division of Christian Education of the National Council of the Churches of Christ in the U.S.A., and used by permission.

The poem "The Autobiography of Gomer" is reproduced herein by permission of its author, Mary Caroline Jonah.

*Book design by Sharon Adams*
*Cover design by Lisa Buckley*
*Cover art:* Abigail and Her Sisters *by Xuereb. Courtesy of SuperStock.*

*First edition*
Published by Westminster John Knox Press
Louisville, Kentucky

This book is printed on acid-free paper that meets the American National Standards Institute Z39.48 standard. ∞

PRINTED IN THE UNITED STATES OF AMERICA

08 09 10 11 12 — 10 9 8 7 6 5

**Library of Congress Cataloging-in-Publication Data**
Sakenfeld, Katharine Doob, 1940–
    Just wives? : stories of power and survival in the Old Testament
    and Today / Katharine Doob Sakenfeld.—1st ed.
        p. cm.
    Includes bibliographical references.
    ISBN-13: 978-0-664-22660-2 (alk. paper)
    ISBN-10: 0-664-22660-4 (alk. paper)
    1. Women in the Bible.    2. Wives—Religious life.    I. Title.

BS575.S25 2004
221.9'22'082—dc21                                                2003050175

# Contents

# Acknowledgments

Those who have shared in the preparation of this book are literally beyond my numbering. They stretch from the rural Philippines to downtown Bangkok, from Africa to Central America, from Kansas and Washington, D.C., to New York and New Jersey. Some are known to me only through their writings; but many hundreds have participated in person, as they have engaged with me in Bible studies in churches, private homes, schools, and continuing education centers. Without their provocative comments and questions this book would be very different or, more likely, not exist at all. I thank them, and I thank God for their witness to the power of these Old Testament stories in their lives.

Four persons must be singled out for special thanks for their role during the writing process. Nyasha Junior has served not only as technical editorial assistant, but also as a challenging voice from a social location different from my own. Stephanie Egnotovich from Westminster John Knox Press believed in this project even before I did and has done much to make the writing clear and lively. Genie Bishop again as in the past made her Vermont retreat available for a time of intense writing. And above all, thanks to my husband, Helmar—his support is a priceless gift for which I am ever grateful. To play on the text for chapter 6 of this book, many have done excellently, but you surpass them all.

# Introduction

I love the story of Ruth!" exclaimed one of the participants with me in a women's Bible study in Asia. "I hate the story of Ruth; I wish I could cut it out of my Bible!" responded another. "Everything was Sarah's fault," argued a woman in my Princeton classroom; "No, Hagar started it," replied another; "Well, what about Abraham!" chimed in a third. "Proverbs 31 is preached every Mother's Day in my church, but I'm not sure I really like that text as well as I used to," reported a student during a discussion of special-day services in local congregations. Moments like these set me on the path to writing this book.

For many years I have listened and learned as women (and some men) from various contexts in North America and in countries across the globe have shared their responses to Old Testament stories about women. Many times my official role in these conversations was teacher, the "expert" in ancient Israelite culture, customs, and literature. But always my role has been colearner, as we sought together to grow in our understanding of these women. Inspired by the different perspectives my colearners brought to the stories, I began to seek out books and articles written by women from various cultural backgrounds, and these too expanded my horizons. No matter where women gather to study these ancient stories, the lives of the women in the Bible have meaning for people in their own situations today.

But what that meaning might be is not the same for everyone, and those differences are the focus of this book. I have had the privilege of teaching in the Philippines and spending time in a half dozen other Asian countries, working always with women studying the Old Testament. Their ideas were often surprising to me as a white, upper-middle-class North American. And through my classes and reading I have been equally challenged by different viewpoints of African-American and Hispanic women within my own home setting. Of course even women from the same background don't always agree about how a story from ancient Israel relates to their situations today! So the discussions are always lively.

In this book I want to introduce you to this lively discussion around some of the Old Testament women, to lead you into the excitement that bubbles up when different views are expressed, and to encourage you to think your own thoughts and even lend your own voice to the ongoing conversation. I hope these women of ancient Israel will come alive for you as never before, that by joining the conversation with women from near at home and around the world you will discover new connections between these women of long ago and your own personal, family, and community concerns today.

From the many possible women in the Old Testament, I have chosen eleven for this book. Sarah and Hagar introduce us to problems that arise when women are unable to conceive, and to tensions surrounding ethnicity and economic status. Ruth and Naomi point us to questions of hunger and starvation, and how marriage does or doesn't fit into women's economic security. Esther and Vashti remind us that even wealth doesn't solve all of women's problems, and show us different strategies for dealing with injustice. Michal, Abigail, and Bathsheba, the three wives of King David, lead us to think about the complexity of human motivation then and now. The story of Gomer, wife of the prophet Hosea, challenges us to consider the impact on her and on women today when God's people are pictured as an unfaithful wife like Gomer. And finally, the poem about the ideal "wife . . . more precious than jewels" in the book of Proverbs invites us to ask what the phrase "good wife" really means, and whether any real-life woman today can meet the standard.

The one thread that links these eleven women is that we know about them primarily in their role as wives, but beyond that they are quite diverse. Obviously the Old Testament has many more stories about wives, but I have chosen this sample to highlight the diversity of their contexts, as well as the relevance of their stories for diverse situations in and beyond marriage. Some of these women are known from narratives, others from prophecy or poetry; some are from Israel's earliest history, others from the middle and end of the Old Testament period; some are queens, others are tent dwellers; some are widows, others are new brides; some appear to have a great deal of power, others appear to have none; some are glad for their marriages, others are quite unhappy; some are idealized in traditional interpretation, others are regarded by tradition as sinners who set a bad example.

Although their lives are different from our lives today, the experiences of these Old Testament women in many ways transcend time and place and raise issues that are highly relevant today to women in North America and also to women globally, as we are all confronted with our own cultural issues, perspectives, and priorities. The diversity of situations and the variety of issues faced by the women I have chosen for study can help us to reflect on our responses to the diverse challenges facing our own lives today.

My approach to the women included in this book combines two main lenses or ways of viewing the texts. My first concern is with the sociocultural background of the biblical material, which means that I ask about and investigate factors in the cultural, economic, religious, and social structures of ancient Israel that may help us to understand practices or activities that seem strange to us today. My second focus is on the literary, or rhetorical, design of a text. This means that I examine the text as we would examine another kind of literature: I consider, for instance, how characters and plot are developed, describe the perspective of the narrator who reports the story, and ask how the meaning of a character's words might change depending on how we imagine the tone of voice. I study the metaphors in a poem, and look at any other concerns that would be associated with a careful study of any piece of good literature.[1]

These two interpretive emphases (sociocultural and literary) have come into the spotlight in biblical interpretation in the past two decades and are much more a feature of recent books and commentaries than of older works. Both these approaches may be used in study of any biblical text; they are not unique to texts about women. By contrast, historical study, which focuses on political events and dates, is not as relevant to these wives and their experiences. That's because the women of the Old Testament, with just a few exceptions, were not involved in the public sphere, even if they were married to public figures such as kings or prophets. In any Bible study, it is important to focus on the lines of inquiry that shed the most light on the questions we bring to the text. Therefore, I do not give much attention to historical questions such as dates and political events.

In this book I make a special effort to share with you some of the ways in which each text is viewed by women in cultures very different from my own predominantly white, upper-middle-class, North American setting. My underlying assumption is that people in very different life circumstances bring different questions to the stories and will see different answers to questions put to the Bible passages. Some of the cross-cultural materials introduced here stem from my own experiences traveling in various parts of Asia and engaging in Bible study with Christian women there. In other cases I draw on books or essays published by women from differing cultural settings around the globe and in North America. Within the North American context, I refer frequently to the perspectives of "womanist"[2] interpreters. These are African-American women scholars in various disciplines whose research and writing include race, gender, and class analysis that gives special attention to the experience of African-American women.

I present the variety and diversity of these different cultural approaches to the texts to help us all explore and recognize that despite great differences, we have similarities as well. I hope readers will feel a new level of empathy and connection to the concerns of women quite different from themselves, and will be challenged to reach out to others. I hope that awareness of differing insights or questions will evoke change in all of us as we face our own circumstances. We will see new possibilities, feel the Spirit stirring in us, hear God's word afresh, so that eventually we will live our lives differently, be transformed, because of knowing what women in very different circumstances have seen in these texts.

Each of the chapters begins with a brief synopsis of the text to be studied, but I hope that you will also have your Bible open to the passage under discussion. This synopsis is designed as a help to the reader, but ideally a Bible should be kept ready at hand. No synopsis or description can be completely "neutral" or "objective," since every summary must select highlights. Indeed, one of my purposes is to show how different interpreters will select different points of emphasis. So readers are encouraged to use the synopses, but not to use them blindly. I encourage each of you to engage the full biblical text carefully and to understand that no question is wrong to ask. At the end of each chapter you will find some questions that can be used for individual reflection or for group discussion. And of course these questions are only starters. In keeping with the spirit of the book itself, I encourage you to generate your own questions and to address the compelling issues of justice, mercy, and faith that these varied Old Testament women raise for your own life today.

## Notes

1. The bringing together of these two emphases may be called a "culturally cued literary approach." The approach is described in more detail in Katharine Doob Sakenfeld, "Feminist Biblical Interpretation," *Theology Today* 46, no. 2 (1989), 154–68.
2. The term "womanist" was coined by African-American author Alice Walker, who conveys her meaning through four dictionary-style definitions in *In Search of Our Mothers' Gardens* (San Diego: Harcourt Brace Jovanovich, 1983), xi–xii. Best known is her description, "Womanist is to feminist as purple to lavender" (xii).

# Chapter One

# Sarah and Hagar: Power and Privileges
## Genesis 16:1–16; 21:1–21

S arah and Hagar are part of the larger story of God's promise to Abraham to provide him with many descendants who will eventually live in a land of their own and become a blessing to others. The Genesis story focuses mainly on the first part of this promise, numerous descendants, but even before the promise is first announced to Abraham (Gen. 12:1–3), readers know that his wife Sarah is childless (Gen. 11:30). How then will the promise be fulfilled? The story of Sarah and Hagar answers this question, but the interaction between them raises a host of other issues important for them and for women today.

In this story we meet a childless woman who longs for the honor and respect accorded to mothers in her society and seeks to remedy her situation. We also meet a female slave who appears to have no options and yet is supported by God in her struggles. We see conflict that arises over a pregnancy compounded by factors of ethnicity and economic status. We meet the mother of Isaac, through whom Jews and Christians trace their relationship to Abraham and God's promises, and we meet the mother of Ishmael, through whom Muslims trace their relationship to Abraham and God's promises. We learn of a God who does not always liberate the oppressed as they would like, but who hears and responds to the cry of the desperate.

Today, even as in ancient Israel, women seek to become mothers, find themselves without options, get caught up in conflicts rooted in ethnicity and economic differences, and are separated by religious heritage. They find that God does not always answer their prayers as they would wish, yet still they find that God does provide. The story of Sarah and Hagar provides a springboard for reflection on these perennial issues.

## The Biblical Story

Sarah (in Gen. 16 she is named Sarai) is unable to bear children to her husband Abraham (in Gen. 16 named Abram). At Sarah's suggestion, Abraham takes Sarah's Egyptian maid Hagar, who becomes pregnant by him. As one might expect, conflict develops between the two women and also between Sarah and Abraham. When Sarah treats Hagar harshly, Hagar runs away to the wilderness, where an angel of the Lord comes to her by a spring of water. The angel instructs Hagar to return to Sarah and also tells her that she will have many offspring through her son, whom she is to name Ishmael ("God hears"). Hagar gives the name El-roi ("God who sees") to the Lord who spoke to her, and when the child is born Abraham gives him the name Ishmael.

In Genesis 17:15–22, the Lord promises Abraham that Sarah will herself bear a son who will be the heir to God's promises to Abraham, although Abraham and Sarah each in turn laugh at the idea that she would become pregnant in her old age (17:17; 18:12).

Despite their laughter, God's promise comes to pass. Sarah does conceive, and she bears Abraham a son whom he names Isaac ("he laughs"). On the day of a party celebrating Isaac's weaning, Sarah sees Ishmael playing with Isaac and asks Abraham to send Hagar and Ishmael away, lest Ishmael share the inheritance with Isaac. Abraham is distressed at the request, but God tells him to send them away; God assures Abraham that although the initial promises are to be fulfilled through Isaac, God will make a great nation of Ishmael's descendants as well. Hagar and Ishmael depart into the wilderness, but their water runs out and the child is about to die. As Hagar weeps, God hears the voice of the boy, and an angel tells Hagar that God will make a great nation of her son. Hagar sees a well of water and gives Ishmael a drink, and God is with the boy as he grows up in the wilderness.

## Growing with the Story

When I first learned part of this story as a kindergartner in a white, small-town, Presbyterian Sunday school, I shared the lesson about Abraham with my mother. She took that occasion to explain to me about my Jewish heritage on one side of my family, and I took it as a matter of great pride to claim this heritage. It was fun to be a relative of somebody important. I used to tell my little friends, "I'm akin to Abraham!"—never knowing that a continent away other children just like me were being put to death in Treblinka and Auschwitz for just that very reason.

Then came the time when I learned part of the larger plot line: Abraham was promised offspring, but Sarah was barren. Finally in their old age Sarah did get pregnant and Isaac was born. So far as I can recall, the Hagar interlude was never mentioned in Sunday school. Probably there were too many potential questions that little kids might ask that would embarrass the teacher. When I did learn about Hagar, her role in the story was downplayed; it was used as evidence that Abraham and especially Sarah lacked faith that God would fulfill the promise of many descendants ("a great nation" [Gen. 12:2]; "offspring [as many as] the dust of the earth" [Gen. 13:16]). Indeed, Sarah received most of the blame, since it was she who suggested the plan of a child by Hagar.

Only much later did someone point out to me that those statements of promise were made just to Abraham. The text never mentions Sarah's presence; nor does it say that Abraham told Sarah about the promises. Thus it is not likely that the text wants to emphasize that Sarah lacks faith when she suggests that Abraham have a child by Hagar. Furthermore, God's early promise of offspring never mentioned who was to be the mother of the many descendants. The role of Sarah as the mother associated with these special promises is not made specific until chapter 17, after Ishmael is born, so even Abraham cannot easily be accused of lack of faith for his actions in chapter 16. In short, although the story builds tension about how God's promise will be fulfilled, it is not necessary for readers of this story to suppose that either Sarah or Abraham showed a lack of trust in God by turning to Hagar. In fact, sending Hagar to Abraham was probably not particularly unusual in their culture (see below). And we ourselves often repeat the expression, "The Lord helps those who help themselves."

Another step in my deeper appreciation of this story came when I noticed that Hagar was an Egyptian (16:1; note that she eventually gets Ishmael an Egyptian wife [21:21], so that references to Egypt frame the entire two-part story). Hagar's ancestry may seem a small point, but it takes on larger significance when viewed in relation to the overall plot lines of Genesis and Exodus and the parallels between them. In the Genesis story, Sarah and Abraham are living in Canaan and Sarah has an Egyptian slave, Hagar, whom she treats harshly. The Egyptian slave first flees to the wilderness but returns, and then later is driven into the wilderness, where God provides water and promises to care for her child. In the book of Exodus we find these events repeated at the level of nations rather than families, except, of course, the roles are reversed. In Exodus the descendants of Abraham and Sarah are living in Egypt and have become slaves of the Egyptians, who treat them harshly. They flee (Exod. 14:5) or are sent away (12:31) into the wilderness, where God supplies them with water and cares for them. I was excited to realize that such a small detail as Hagar's ancestry could have such impact on my understanding of the story of Sarah and Hagar in the larger biblical setting.

Then in 1988 I participated in a conference in which Jewish, Muslim, and African-American Christian women spoke on the story of Sarah and Hagar. In the course of that conference I found a hero I'd never imagined.[1] First the Muslim speaker lauded Hagar as the progenitress through Ishmael of the Arab and Muslim community worldwide. Then the African-American speaker claimed Hagar for her community with reference to a long folkloric and musical heritage from the nineteenth-century slavery and subsequent Jim Crow era, a heritage that I would never have guessed existed. And the Jewish speaker suggested that all the problems between Sarah and Hagar really should be laid at the feet of Abraham and the male-dominated system in which they lived. Disagreement among the presenters grew heated and was further fueled by probing and sometimes antagonistic questions from a multicultural, multiracial, religiously plural audience, many of whom were uncomfortable with new and unfamiliar interpretations of the main characters. The biblical story suddenly took on new significance for me. Hagar, a minor character in my own white Protestant tradition, was more central than Sarah in the traditions of others.

In recent years writers in both church and academic circles have begun to view Hagar and Sarah as full characters, rather than just as vessels for providing Abraham's offspring. Contributions to this discussion range from Phyllis Trible's literary reading in her volume *Texts of Terror*[2] to the womanist[3] thematic approaches by Delores Williams in *Sisters in the Wilderness*[4] and Renita Weems in *Just a Sister Away*,[5] to a technical work on kinship patterns by Naomi Steinberg.[6] They include essays by Oh Soo Hae,[7] a Japanese woman of Korean descent, and Elsa Tamez,[8] Old Testament scholar and past president of La Universidad Bíblica Latinoamericana in Costa Rica. The variety of perspectives and approaches is fascinating and challenging. It is not possible to treat all the interpretations here, or even to summarize them. I hope rather to encourage you to look more closely at this biblical story by considering four of the themes and issues these authors have raised: (1) sociocultural responses to barrenness, (2) the conflict between Sarah and Hagar, (3) God's command that Hagar return to Sarah, and (4) God's promise to Hagar.

## Barrenness

Having children, especially sons, was of central importance in Israel's culture, as it was in other surrounding cultures and still is in most cultures today. (Sons have the privilege and responsibility of carrying on the family name and inheriting the family property.) Thus societies in every era have developed sociocultural patterns to deal with barrenness. Adoption, the solution most familiar to people today, is only one of a number of approaches. Abraham had actually considered adopting one of his male slaves as his legal heir, but God had promised him a son born to him (Gen. 15:3–4). In some cultures serial monogamy is an alternative to adoption. In this system, the husband divorces his barren wife and remarries in the hope that the new wife will produce children. Still another way to deal with barrenness is by the practice of polygyny, in which the husband marries additional wives of equal status.

The Sarah-Hagar-Abraham relationship represents yet another option for dealing with barrenness—the practice called polycoity, in which a husband takes an additional wife who has secondary (rather than equal) status with his first wife.[9] Sarah's plan, accepted by Abraham, to have children through a polycoity arrangement was probably not unusual in their culture. The distinction between polygyny and polycoity is important: in polycoity the primary wife has more power than the secondary wife. Thus when Hagar is given to Abraham she is not promoted to full or equal wife status alongside Sarah. Rather, Hagar is classified as a "secondary wife," a more meaningful description for most modern readers than the technical "concubine." The difference in power between the two women that begins with the mistress-slave relationship continues as Hagar becomes the secondary wife, and it fuels the conflict between the women that we will consider in the next section.

Although in polycoity the additional wife has secondary status, a son born to the secondary wife is regarded as the primary heir to the land and property of his father, unless the primary wife later bears a son, which, of course, does not usually happen. It did happen, however, in the Sarah-Hagar story: Sarah, the primary wife, bore Isaac, who at his birth became entitled to the full inheritance. Ishmael's status then dropped to the same secondary status as his mother; he was no longer entitled to any property or inheritance.

But Sarah worried nonetheless that Ishmael might usurp Isaac's status (21:10) and therefore urged Abraham to send Hagar and Ishmael away. Perhaps the Old Testament custom governing this issue was not well established in Israel. Or perhaps Sarah's worry reveals the depth of her concern for her own status. For in a culture such as Israel's, it was important for a woman not just to be a mother, but to be the mother of a son, and more specifically to be the mother of the son who would be the father's heir.

While these events and practices in Genesis may seem like historical relics to many twenty-first-century Americans, stories from women in modern Africa remind us that various options and practices regarding infertility are not simply a matter of bygone times. I recall an African student whose husband had divorced her and whose family had ostracized her because she had been unable to conceive. None of the technological medical expertise available to well-insured North American women had been available to her; it was simply assumed by the extended families on both sides that the "fault" (an appropriate term in this story) was hers. Coming to study in the United States, in the midst of a culture with such completely different strategies for dealing with barrenness, had only exacerbated this woman's emotional pain. Unlikely as it might seem to many American readers, she might have been glad for the option available to Sarah, despite its risks.

In another African context, the Shona society (found in present-day Zimbabwe and parts of Zambia and Mozambique), arrangements are made for a wife who has not conceived to have intercourse with one of her husband's brothers. If she still does not conceive, it is determined that the fault is hers. In the era before European colonization of Africa, Shona society had a traditional practice in place for overcoming such barrenness: the bride's extended family chose a younger girl, usually a sister or niece of the bride, to live with the new couple from the very beginning. It was understood that if the wife did not bear a child, this younger woman would do so on her behalf. If, as was more usually the case, the wife did bear children, then the wife was also responsible for rearing the younger sister and finding her a suitable husband. Today this practice is generally no longer followed. The husband now seeks another wife and the barren first wife must decide whether to stay with him or not.[10]

Dora Mbuwayesango, an Old Testament scholar from Africa, compares these Shona traditions to the story of Sarah. She points out that both cultures seem to associate woman's worth primarily with the bearing of children. Although the Shona culture does not automatically assume that the fault for barrenness lies with the woman, in both cases childless women are stigmatized, and arrangements must be made to provide a child when the first wife is barren.[11]

The cultural importance of childbearing, especially of a male child, is central to the biblical story and remains powerful in our own time as well. The text reveals that in offering Hagar to Abraham Sarah has her own interests at heart at least as much as his, if not more so. Sarah hopes she will "obtain children by [Hagar]" (16:2; translated literally, Sarah hopes to be "built up"). To speak aloud to her husband the words "the LORD has prevented me from bearing children" (16:2) would surely have meant heart-wrenching anguish for Sarah, and to propose that he have a child by Hagar would further have reinforced her own sense of incompleteness, whatever her demeanor before Abraham may have been.

The experiences of women in our own society who are unable to conceive can help to sensitize us to the emotional pain lying behind Sarah's decision. All the thoughtless questions from others—"When are you going to . . ." or "Why haven't you . . ." or "Have you tried . . ."—and all the private soul-searching of "Why me?" start us on the track toward appreciating Sarah's feelings. In Sarah's case, she believed that God had deliberately, for some unknown reason, "prevented" her from bearing children. What must it have been like to believe that God had deliberately done this to her? (And surely some women believe that today.) How ambivalent women who are unable to conceive must be toward the end of Sarah's story—and Hannah's story (1 Sam. 1–2) and the stories of other biblical women whose barrenness is eventually overcome while theirs today is not.

Various news stories about women in the United States who seek out surrogate mothers make clear from another perspective that the story of Sarah and Hagar is not simply an ancient one, or one with contemporary resonances only in non-Western cultures. While the social stigma of childlessness may have diminished, the deep desire for offspring still remains. The motives of women who desire children yet are unable to bear them may or may not resemble Sarah's, but outsiders can scarcely know either the details of the inner desires or the cultural and personal pressures upon such women.

Likewise, outsiders cannot know fully the variety of motives of the women who make themselves available as surrogates. Grandmothers have carried their own grandchildren on behalf of their daughters; women have offered to carry another's child for pay; women have volunteered out of kindness and empathy for others. We know that in a number of cases the woman who carried the child has been emotionally unable or unwilling to give up the newborn child to its "real" mother, and tensions similar to those between Hagar and Sarah have arisen. The complexity of emotions in such cases is almost beyond imagining.

As we recognize the deep emotions surrounding surrogacy today, it is essential to observe that we know nothing of Hagar's feelings about being given to Abraham. There is some evidence that Hagar's status may have been increased among other slaves by this circumstance, and especially by her pregnancy. Yet it is not clear whether Hagar welcomed this change. Delores Williams has drawn a parallel between Hagar's treatment and the pattern of forced surrogacy in the slaveholding era of the United States. Despite the evidence that black women did not submit willingly to the sexual advances of their white masters, the white community created a myth to excuse the behavior of these men and ignore the exploitation of these slaves—the myth of the oversexed, erotic, and eagerly responsive African woman that persists to this day in many circles.[12]

## Conflict between Sarah and Hagar

A second theme that demands our attention is the conflict between Sarah and Hagar. The two women were divided from one another both by ethnicity (one a Hebrew, the other an Egyptian), and by economic class (Sarah as the one with relative economic power, Hagar dependent upon her as slave who had to our knowledge no personal economic resources).

Economic standing is not everything, however, and once Hagar conceives she has the one thing that Sarah cannot achieve—the honor that is ascribed to a pregnant woman in a society that values and needs children so highly, and especially the honor that comes from carrying the child of the head of the household. Sarah may not have anticipated that Hagar's attitude would change if she became pregnant, or she may have just decided the risk was worth it; moreover, we do not know anything of the relationship between Sarah and Hagar before Hagar was given to Abraham.

For whatever reason, once Hagar conceives, "her mistress was slight in her eyes" (16:4, Phyllis Trible's translation).[13] Sarah now faults Abraham for this turn of events—he who had only concurred in what Sarah had suggested. Abraham, however, insists that Sarah deal with her own slave as she sees fit, a clear indication that Hagar's formally subordinate status has not changed. And so, Sarah deals harshly (16:6) with Hagar, who flees into the wilderness. Hagar subseqently returns and both Ishmael and Isaac are born. But after some years Sarah feels threatened again, this time over inheritance rights for her son. She says to Abraham, "Cast out this slave woman with her son; for the son of this slave woman shall not inherit along with my son Isaac" (21:10). With Abraham's cooperation—and with God's reassurance to Abraham—Hagar and Ishmael are driven out of their lives and into the wilderness.

Womanist Old Testament scholar Renita Weems draws upon the history of slavery in America to interpret the conflict between these biblical women, affirming the truth of the observation that "to be under the power of a resentful woman can be a dangerous thing."[14] Although slavery was abolished nearly 140 years ago, its memories and attitudes, its pain and antagonisms are still much with us. Weems reminds us that even today most black women in America "carry a footlocker of hurtful memories of encounters with white women."[15] Often white women unthinkingly describe their experience as though it were universal, denying in the process the different experiences of African-American and other women in their very midst who are not like themselves. Weems gives poignant examples of the ways in which, despite her established career and her educational and academic credentials, she is frequently still treated like Hagar in encounters with white women. She points to the modern counterparts of class differences in our story as well—Sarah is the wife of a wealthy landowner, Hagar her lowly maid—and notes that across the globe groups of women are locked into struggles against other women, rather than alongside of them. Forcefully and poignantly she insists that "injustice in our lands relies upon the perpetual alienation of women from one another and upon relentless hostility between women."[16]

This theme of injustice and alienation is picked up in quite a different cultural setting by Oh Soo Hae, a woman of Korean descent who grew up in Japan. Japan is not a homogeneous society, despite its popular image as such among both Japanese and outsiders. Among the minority groups are the Okinawans, the Ainu, the *burakumin* (who are literally untouchables and actually Japanese), and the Koreans whose forebears were brought to Japan as conscripted labor several generations ago. Oh Soo Hae is one of these Koreans. She details Japanese government policies that until recently both required cultural Japanization and denied citizenship rights and voting privileges to these third- and fourth-generation residents. Gang hazing of their children at school remained common, and families had little access to housing and credit. In Asia in the early 1990s I met with some of these Korean women and heard their stories. On our visit to the Hiroshima Peace Park they pointed out that the monument to the Koreans who died at Hiroshima had to be erected by the Korean community outside the park; it was not allowed to be on the official park grounds. Oh Soo Hae identified herself with Hagar as she wrote:

> Ever since I can remember I have been asking God why God created me a Korean. Why did God see fit to allow me to face such suffering? To be so depressed about my situation that I even considered taking my own life? In the end, the meaning of our existence lies in our being used to raise the level of understanding among our Japanese neighbors. Realizing that truth, I found my identity. . . . As the Koreans in Japan are liberated, the Japanese will be liberated with them.[17]

Oh Soo Hae cannot undo the fact of her Korean heritage in a context of Japanese prejudice. But she finds her Christian identity in working together with other Koreans and sensitized Japanese women to challenge such prejudice with the message that God's blessing surely is for all people.[18]

The purpose of paying attention to such stories from outside our immediate cultural context is not only to become educated about oppression and suffering in other parts of our own society or other parts of the world, although that is a beneficial and necessary first step. But we also need to hear these stories in order to find our own place more clearly in the biblical story and in our own cultural contexts. Learning where other contemporary women find themselves and their people should sharpen our own imaginative connections to the pain and the possibilities of the story.

### Return, Submit: God's Command to Hagar

The most difficult aspect of the story of Hagar for many readers is the first part of the encounter between Hagar and the angel of the Lord in the wilderness, as recorded in Genesis 16:8–9:

> And he said, "Hagar, slave-girl of Sarai, where have you come from and where are you going?" She said, "I am running away from my mistress Sarai." The angel of the LORD said to her, "Return to your mistress, and submit to her."

"Return, submit!" What kind of God would give a command like that? Many readers get stuck here, I among them, as we recall what Hagar's life was like before. Sarah "dealt harshly" with her (the same word that is used to describe how the Egyptians later treated the Israelite slaves in Egypt), which in Weems's words would have meant "beatings, verbal insults, ridicule, strenuous work, degrading tasks."[19] Is a God who gives such a command worthy of our worship?

Before we turn to interpretations that address the difficulty many of us experience in facing this text, we need to remember that not all readers in all times have reacted with dismay to this command. White American slaveholders in the mid-1800s, for example, had quite a different view. The command to Hagar,

"Return, submit," was exactly what they would have hoped and, in fact, expected that God would say to recalcitrant, runaway slaves. According to their reading of Genesis 9, Hagar the Egyptian was African, a descendant of Ham, destined for subjection to Sarah, just as their African slaves were in subjection. Hagar was not fully human, according to their anthropology, so she didn't really have feelings like white folk and she could not have the maturity and resourcefulness to manage on her own; thus she needed to return for her own good, and of course for the economic good of her master and mistress. Besides, Hagar was carrying the master's child. That child was of great economic value, even if Hagar herself was expendable. So for the slaveholders God's command to "return, submit" confirmed their view of the order of creation concerning other races, their view of Hagar as an individual, their sense of their own economic needs, and their desire for family stability.

Just as interpretations of biblical stories from other contemporary cultures challenge us to examine our own lives, so we should try to learn from an interpretation of the story such as this, one that comes from our own past. Who are the folk around us whom we still consider inferior, slightly less in the image of God than ourselves and the people more like us? Who are the runaways from contemporary social structures to whom we are expecting God to say, "Return, submit"? Illegal aliens? Supporters of the spotted owl or some other endangered species? Gays and lesbians? Allegedly inefficient small-acreage farmers? Street people? Perhaps even persons of other racial-ethnic groups? According to a traditional saying, "New occasions teach new duties."[20] As we in principle side with Hagar in her plight, we may unwittingly in our actual behavior be siding with Sarah. God's will for justice, peace, and the integrity of creation is not yet fully clear to us.

What, then, can we say about this difficult command "Return, submit"? Why isn't the slave Hagar offered the same liberation from her personal oppression that God gives to the Israelites later on? It is hard to understand how the God we know from so many parts of the Bible as the God of justice and deliverance could deny such liberation to Hagar.

One approach to answering this troubling question suggests that the stories in Genesis 16 and 21 are really two variant versions of the same story handed down through long oral tradition. If this is the case, then the compiler of the stories in our book of Genesis needed to have Hagar return to Sarah so that both versions of the story could be retained. The preservation of varying versions of important community traditions is a practice well attested in many cultures. And, in fact, certain similarities between the two stories in chapters 16 and 21 do point in this direction:

1. Sarah becomes discontented and approaches Abraham about it (16:5; 21:9–10).
2. Hagar ends up in the wilderness (16:6; 21:14).
3. God (or the angel of God) addresses Hagar in the wilderness (16:7–12; 21:17–18).
4. God gives a promise concerning Hagar's son (16:10; 21:13, 18).
5. A reference is made to a well in the wilderness (16:7, 14; 21:19).

In many respects this hypothesis of alternative versions of the story is compelling. Nonetheless, this explanation does not directly interpret the narrative as it was eventually passed down as literature and as Scripture, in which the relationship between Sarah and Hagar is presented as having two stages. Nor does the hypothesis of alternative versions address our primary concern here, namely the discomfort we experience with God's command to Hagar to "return, submit." Readers who view the Bible as Scripture must still struggle with these words, regardless of how they came to be included.

Another approach takes account of the two stages by offering a human rationale for God's words: God told Hagar to return for her own good. After all, how could a pregnant woman survive in the wilderness? But this explanation has its problems as well. A God who provides water and manna for the Israelites in their wilderness wandering could surely do as much for one Egyptian slave seeking her freedom. Indeed, God does provide water for Hagar at the end of the second episode, in chapter 21. Somehow, God could have helped Hagar to survive her initial flight from Sarah. God's command to Hagar seems to undercut the idea of a God who offers liberation and freedom, a basic Old Testament theme.

In response to this concern, womanist theologian Delores Williams has offered a different perspective that places God's command in a broader context. Williams uses the story of Hagar as the biblical starting point for developing her womanist "god-talk" (that is, theological reflection), precisely because of the many parallels between Hagar's story and African-American women's historical and current experience. Rather than focus primarily or initially on liberation, however, as do many white feminists, black male theologians, and indeed other womanist theologians, Williams identifies survival and quality of life as her key themes.

Thus Williams can deal with Genesis 16 on its own terms and write, "The angel of Yahweh is, in this passage, no liberator God."[21] God's command does not provide liberation, but it does ensure survival for mother and child. Survival and quality of life are linked for Williams here, because mother and child will be not only provided for, but well provided for in the camp of wealthy Abraham.[22]

Williams does not discount liberationist concerns, but she sees the African-American community's theological question about survival and quality of life as equally important. She struggles mightily with the question of why God said, "Return, submit." Although she sees that the text appears to present God siding with Sarah, not with Hagar, she knows there is a long history of hope associated with Hagar's story among her African-American people. She writes:

> The truth of the matter may well be that the Bible gives license for us to have it both ways: God liberates and God does not always liberate the oppressed. God speaks comforting words to the survival and quality-of-life struggle of many families.[23]

Williams's insistence that God is at work in both liberation and survival suggests two themes for ongoing reflection in relation to God's command to Hagar to "return, submit." First, since it is unlikely that racism, sexism, or economic exploitation will disappear in the near future, our theology needs to have room for God to be at work supporting and caring about those who are oppressed within these structures from which there is no apparent escaping. God is present and at work in the struggle for survival and some degree of quality of life within all the brokenness of this world. Those who are well off should not criticize those whose struggle for survival leaves them no time or energy for thinking about liberation.

Second, and on the other hand, a theology of survival is needed primarily for those circumstances in which God helps people, as Williams says, to "make a way out of no way."[24] For those of us in a position of relative power and privilege, the danger is that a theology of survival may lull us back into the Sarah role. We may be tempted to continue in personal and systemic behaviors that perpetuate oppression, looking only to our own existence and not seeking to identify and participate in God's liberating action on behalf of others. The angel of God directed Hagar toward survival, but our discomfort with that command requires us to work for liberation.

### Many Descendants: God's Promise to Hagar

The final theme for our consideration, also from Hagar's wilderness experience, follows directly upon God's command to Hagar to return to Sarah. Hagar, the first woman in the Bible to whom God or God's angel appears, is now given a great promise, the same promise given to Abraham a few chapters earlier (13:16; 15:5):

> "I will so greatly multiply your offspring that they cannot be counted for multitude." (16:10)

Hagar is told to name her son Ishmael ("God hears") because the Lord has given heed to (heard) her affliction (16:11). After the angel speaks, we are told that Hagar "named the LORD who spoke to her, 'You are El-roi [God who sees]'" (16:13). While many biblical persons give a name to the place where they encounter God, Hagar here actually names God rather than the place of meeting. Ishmael, God hears; El-roi, God sees. These same two verbs of hearing and seeing by which God is in touch with Hagar's affliction appear together again in the turning point of the Exodus story:

> The Israelites groaned under their slavery, and cried out. . . . God heard their groaning. . . . God looked upon [lit. "saw"] the Israelites. (Exod. 2:23–25)

How much better most Christians know the story of the Israelites than the story of Hagar. How much more easily most of us identify with the dramatic deliverance at the Red Sea than with the flight or later the driving out of a single slave woman whose offspring became the ancestor of some other people. How much we rely upon our connection to the words of Exodus 2:24: "God remembered his covenant with Abraham, Isaac, and Jacob."

"I'm akin to Abraham." My childhood claim is not restricted to those of Jewish descent. Gentile Christians understand themselves to be ingrafted into Abraham but the focus is on Abraham's lineage through Isaac. And so, despite our sometimes good intentions, many of us Christians tend to forget about Hagar and her story. We forget her pain, her courage, her resistance to mistreatment, her naming of the God of survival and of liberation. We forget that her son, Ishmael, God Hears, also became the progenitor of a great people, and is revered by Arabs and Muslims today as their great ancestor and link to Abraham.

Next time you hear about Abraham, remember Sarah, and when you remember Sarah, remember Hagar. Remember that in Hagar God has affirmed the marginalized in their desire to be included in history.[25] Remember so that you will be more open to those not like yourself. Remember so that your heart will be opened to the outcast and downtrodden. Remember so that you will believe that God sees and hears, that the cry of one lonely and fearful person in the wilderness does not go unheard.

## Questions for Individual Reflection or Group Study

1. When did you first learn the story of Sarah and Hagar? If you have known it for some time, recall your own history of growing in your knowledge about it. What were turning points for you?
2. What is your experience with women who are unable to conceive? How may God be at work (or not) in their lives?
3. How have concerns about stepchildren, blended families, or surrogate motherhood affected your life?
4. Make a list of positive character traits you would assign to Sarah, and another list you would assign to Hagar. Make a list of negative traits for each. Where does the biblical story suggest these traits to you? What traits, if any, do the two women have in common? How are you like either or both of these women?
5. What is your experience of interaction with women of ethnic groups or economic class different from your own? What tensions have arisen? In what ways may differences in power and privilege have affected the interaction?
6. How do the need for survival and the need for liberation relate to your life? Is one more important than the other for you? How do you experience God at work enabling survival and offering liberation?
7. Do you think God hears and sees people in their distress and afflictions today? If so, does it make a difference in their lives?

### Notes

1. Conference on Race, Gender, and Class: Implications for Interpreting Religious Texts, Princeton Theological Seminary, 1988. Proceedings available as sound recording, Reigner Media Area, Princeton Theological Seminary.
2. Phyllis Trible, *Texts of Terror: Literary-Feminist Readings of Biblical Narratives* (Philadelphia: Fortress Press, 1984).
3. See the Introduction for further explanation of the term "womanist."
4. Delores S. Williams, *Sisters in the Wilderness: The Challenge of Womanist God-Talk* (Maryknoll, N.Y.: Orbis Books, 1993).

5. Renita J. Weems, *Just a Sister Away: A Womanist Vision of Women's Relationships in the Bible* (San Diego: LuraMedia, 1988).

6. Naomi Steinberg, *Kinship and Marriage in Genesis: A Household Economics Perspective* (Minneapolis: Fortress Press, 1993).

7. Oh Soo Hae, "The Story of Two Women," in *Women of Courage: Asian Women Reading the Bible* (ed. Oo Chung Lee et al.; Seoul, Korea: Asian Women's Resource Centre for Culture and Theology, 1992).

8. Elsa Tamez, "The Woman Who Complicated the History of Salvation," in *New Eyes for Reading: Biblical and Theological Reflections by Women from the Third World* (ed. John S. Pobee and Bärbel von Wartenberg-Potter; Geneva: World Council of Churches, 1986).

9. Steinberg, *Kinship and Marriage*, 61–68.

10. Dora Rudo Mbuwayesango, "Childlessness and Woman-to-Woman Relationships in Genesis and in African Patriarchal Society: Sarah and Hagar from a Zimbabwean Woman's Perspective (Gen 16:1–16; 21:8–12)," in *Reading the Bible as Women: Perspectives from Africa, Asia, and Latin America* (ed. Phyllis Bird; Atlanta: Scholars Press, 1997), 28–29.

11. Ibid., 34.

12. Williams, *Sisters in the Wilderness*, 70.

13. Trible, *Texts of Terror*, 12. The NRSV translation (Hagar "looked with contempt on" Sarah) assumes a much more negative connotation for the Hebrew phrase.

14. Weems, *Just a Sister Away*, 6.

15. Ibid., 8.

16. Ibid., 18.

17. Hae, "The Story of Two Women," 83.

18. Ibid.

19. Weems, *Just a Sister Away*, 6.

20. See James Russell Lowell, "Present Crisis," in *Yale Book of American Verse* (ed. Thomas R. Lounsbury; New Haven, Conn.: Yale University Press, 1913), 281.

21. Williams, *Sisters in the Wilderness*, 21.

22. Ibid.

23. Ibid., 199.

24. Ibid., 6.

25. Tamez, "The Woman Who Complicated the History of Salvation," 17.

# Chapter Two

# Ruth and Naomi:
# Economic Survival and Family Values
# Ruth 1–4

Today much of church conversation seems to be about sex and money. These two topics, in an ancient cultural form, are also central to the book of Ruth, and at one level the issue of economic survival drives the plot of the book of Ruth. Although the book of Ruth can be approached from many perspectives, we will focus primarily on the connection between economic survival and family values.[1] As Ruth and Naomi, despite tension in their relationship, work together for their economic survival, they devise a plan that moves outside the boundaries of sexual propriety in their culture. Circumstances force them to make difficult decisions in relation to the family values of their culture, just as happens to many women today.

## The Biblical Story

Naomi, her husband, and her two sons reside in Bethlehem. When a famine strikes their village, the family migrates to Moab, where the two sons marry Moabite women, Ruth and Orpah. Naomi's husband and sons die, leaving the three widowed women alone. Naomi hears that God has provided food in Bethlehem and decides to return home. She urges her daughters-in-law to return to their own families, but Ruth insists on accompanying her mother-in-law to Bethlehem. Upon arriving in Bethlehem, Naomi tells the village women to call her "Mara," which means "bitter," because "the Almighty has dealt bitterly" with her (1:20).

Immediately Naomi and Ruth need food, and Ruth goes out to glean. She comes to the field of Boaz, the most prominent citizen of the village, who treats her kindly. Naomi sees the hand of God at work in their encounter, for Boaz is one of her dead husband's relatives.

Time passes. Naomi announces that she needs to "seek some security" for Ruth (3:1) and proposes a plan for Ruth to approach Boaz on the threshing floor during the night and then follow Boaz's lead. Ruth agrees, but when the actual encounter with Boaz takes place, Ruth herself takes the initiative in the conversation, in effect proposing that they be married. Boaz is not resistant to the idea but replies that there is a nearer kinsman, another man in the village who is first in line for such a responsibility; Boaz will marry Ruth if that man does not.

In a meeting of the town elders, Boaz explains the situation to the nearer kinsman, who declares that he is not in a position to marry Ruth. Boaz then announces that he will marry her. The men of the village offer words of blessing to Boaz, concentrating on the fertility of his bride, the marriage is consummated, and a boy Obed is born to Ruth. The village women bless God for the arrival of Obed, telling Naomi that he will be "a restorer of life and a nourisher of your old age; for your daughter-in-law who loves you, who is more to you than seven sons, has borne him" (4:15). The story concludes with the information that baby Obed grew up to become the grandfather of King David.

## The Story of Kamla

Before considering Ruth as a story of economic survival and family values, let's look at the quite different but ultimately related story of Kamla, a story based on the actual experiences of young girls in Thailand. The story appears in a book prepared for use with sixth-graders in rural Thailand.[2] Kamla was the daughter of a village family of tenant farmers in rural Thailand, the youngest child in a large family whose rice paddy, like the others of their village, produced too little rice to feed the entire family. Her education ended at grade 6, the limit of free schooling. When her father became ill the next year, the family debts mounted, so Kamla found a job in a restaurant in a nearby town. She received room, food, and U.S. $0.40 per day for working nearly twenty hours a day. One day, dizzy from exhaustion, she dropped her tray, smashing the plates and bowls. The furious owner dismissed her on the spot, and she was forced to work at odd jobs. Her family, of course, remained in debt.

One day Kaeo, a former classmate who worked in Bangkok, came home to visit. Kaeo was well dressed and had brought home a tape recorder for her family. Kamla, too, could get work in a home in Bangkok to help her family, Kaeo told her. A month later, Kaeo returned and this time brought her boss, Mae Chan, to visit Kamla and her family. Mae Chan, dressed in gold and diamonds, offered Kamla's parents U.S. $1,200.00 as an advance on their daughter's wages and promised to send more each month. Dazzled, the parents agreed, and Mae Chan took Kamla to Bangkok on a first-class, air-conditioned bus.

Perhaps you can guess the rest of the story. Kamla was taken to a brothel and forced to serve as an underage prostituted child.[3] She was not cooperative, so she was beaten and guarded lest she try to escape. Isolated lockup and deprivation of food and water were weapons of the brothel owner. Communication with her family was impossible. One night, as she lighted incense sticks and prayed to be rescued, the building in which she was imprisoned caught fire from the incense sticks, and she and the other girls died in the flames.

This story from Thailand has its counterparts in country after country around the globe, including the United States. The book from which I took the story was prepared by an organization that works to warn rural families of the real intentions of the "recruiters" who come to their villages. Kamla's is a story about economic survival; it is also a story about family values, as it raises questions about the place of girl children in the family structure, about appropriate and safe sexual behavior, and about the role of parents as well as the girls themselves in making such decisions.

Keep this story in mind as we turn to the book of Ruth, for the times have changed but the issues have not. We will see a progression of survival issues as we move through the story of Ruth, and I will discuss them in relation to the story sequence. I will follow the traditional chapter divisions of the book of Ruth and will focus on four issues: famine and desperation; short-term solutions; long-term planning; marriage and control of property in the family. At the end of the chapter we will consider God's role in the story of Ruth and how human responsibility is related to God's role.

### Ruth 1: Famine and Desperation

> There was a famine in the land, and a certain man of Bethlehem in Judah went to live in the country of Moab. (Ruth 1:1)

The scene is set very quickly, in just these two phrases, but apart from the famine the story would never have unfolded. Migration because of famine is certainly known in other parts of the Bible as well. The most familiar examples are in Genesis, where first Abraham goes from Canaan to Egypt (Gen. 12:10), then Isaac goes to Gerar (apparently in the area of Gaza; Gen. 26:1), and later Jacob's sons seek food in Egypt and the family eventually migrates to Egypt (Gen. 42–43; 46).

The ancient Israelites sometimes viewed famine as a judgment from God. We see this, for example, in the focus on crop failures from drought and insect plagues in the list of dire consequences for covenant disobedience given as a warning to Israel:

> You shall carry much seed into the field but shall gather little in, for the locust shall consume it. You shall plant vineyards and dress them, but you shall neither drink the wine nor gather the grapes, for the worm shall eat them. You shall have olive trees throughout all your territory, but you shall not anoint yourself with the oil, for your olives shall drop off. . . . All your trees and the fruit of your ground the cicada shall take over. (Deut. 28:38–42)

The story of the prophet Elijah and the widow's last oil and flour (1 Kgs. 17) is yet another example of this general concern in the Old Testament, a concern common also throughout the ancient world, where the threat of famine was ever present. For those living in a subsistence agrarian economy such as that of an Israelite village, the Genesis story of Joseph in Egypt storing up seven years' worth of food in anticipation of a famine (Gen. 41) would have been quite unrealistic. That much surplus could not have been grown or stored, nor was there a means to transport large amounts of food long distances from one location to another.

In such subsistence cultures, migration in search of food has always been a matter of the most fundamental economic survival. As we look across the globe today, we know that such migration for survival remains a fact of life for many people. In 2002 it is particularly frequent in Afghanistan and in countries of southern Africa such as Angola, Zambia, and Malawi. Drought is forcing mass migrations of people in these regions, migrations that are sometimes even greater in scope than political refugee migrations in the face of civil and tribal strife.

But migration in search of economic survival takes place even when there is not immediate and widespread famine. The migration of African-American sharecroppers in the United States from southern farmlands to northern urban centers during the twentieth century is another manifestation of the search for economic survival. Hong Kong, a wealthy oasis adjacent to the much poorer mainland of China, is just one of many cities across the globe that has experienced an influx of economic refugees. The effort of many governments, including certainly the United States, to resist such migration, to limit the influx of immigrants seeking to escape joblessness and poverty in their homelands, is another modern aspect of this age-old problem.

It has puzzled scholars that in the story of Ruth, Naomi's family migrated to the country of Moab, for most of Moab received even less rainfall on average than Canaan. Although we are not told the cause of the "famine in the land" (1:1) in the story of Ruth, only certain parts of Moab could have a miniclimate different enough from the Bethlehem area to avoid suffering from the same drought. It may be that the narrator designates Moab not because it was fertile territory but because it was regarded as one of Israel's most hated enemies.

In fact, Israel's hostile attitude toward Moab intensifies many themes in the story. As a silent backdrop, this hostility should be kept in mind in interpreting all that takes place: the unspoken explanation of the deaths of Naomi's husband and sons (who went to enemy land); the unspoken rationale for Naomi's preference to return home without her Moabite daughters-in-law (a potential embarrassment to her); the magnitude of Ruth's decision to accompany Naomi (traveling to an enemy land); the attitude of the male reapers toward Ruth (an easily exploitable enemy woman); the magnanimity of Boaz (who is kind to a woman from enemy territory); and the message for ethnic and cultural inclusiveness that even King David was not of "pure" Israelite stock. Whatever the reason for the choice of Moab as the destination, the theme of migration in search of economic survival sets the stage.

### Ruth 2: Short-Term Solutions

Naomi returned home because "she had heard in the country of Moab that the LORD had considered his people and given them food" (1:6). But the availability of food in general does not necessarily mean that any particular family eats regularly. So Ruth must go out to glean. The laws in Leviticus 19:9–10; 23:22 and Deuteronomy 24:19–22 specify arrangements and rules for gleaning. The basic rule was that the edges of the field should not be harvested, and the "gleanings," that is, what was not picked up in the first pass-through of those who bundle the grain-stalks, should be left behind for the alien (Lev. 19:10; 23:22; Deut. 24:19), the poor (Lev. 19:10; 23:22), the orphan, and the widow (Deut. 24:19). As a poor alien widow, Ruth seeks out this means of survival designated for her by Israelite law.

Because Boaz looks favorably on Ruth (whether because she is attractive or because he admires her loyalty to Naomi), he sees to it that extra grain is placed in her path (2:16), an opportunity not available to other gleaners. The harvesters include both women and men, and the risks of gleaning are made apparent as Boaz urges Ruth to stick near the women and keep her eyes down, and as he orders the young men not to "bother" Ruth (2:9; the Jewish Publication Society translates this verb as "molest," indicating its possible negative sexual connotation). Gleaners are the poorest of the poor, and this was especially the case for women on their own such as Naomi and Ruth, who had to take risks to survive.

Gleaning is a short-term solution, however, because the harvest season itself is short. We do not know for sure, but it seems unlikely that gleaning could have provided enough surplus food to sustain an individual or family from one harvest season to the next. A contemporary comparison to the system of gleaning as a short-term solution is the welfare structures offered to the poor by the U.S. government, whereby special forms of financial support are made available to the destitute or the unemployed. Of course modern government bureaucracies are vastly different from ancient Israelite villages, but the concept of the society as a whole providing a "safety net" is reminiscent of the ancient gleaning provisions. Both the ancient Israelite system and the modern governmental systems are intended to prevent starvation for needy people, but neither structure leads in itself to economic self-sufficiency. Poverty is not ended. And now as in ancient times, it is disproportionately women and children who must make use of these structures.

Yet today in most of the so-called third or two-thirds world, the poorest countries and continents, there are no such governmental structures. In rural areas, many people still glean after the mechanical harvesters of large-scale farming have passed through. Others manage to plant subsistence crops in the narrow spaces alongside railroad beds or in other unlikely spots. Still others must resort to "poaching" in areas where gleaning is forbidden or impractical.

The city version of gleaning is even more tragic. In metropolitan Manila in the Philippines, for instance, over two million of a population of about nine million live without running water or sanitary sewer facilities. No square foot of space between buildings is left unoccupied. Much of a squatter's meager income from odd jobs or begging goes to pay off the police so that their cardboard dwelling will not be dismantled. Family structure is directly affected, as responsibility for the family's economic survival is assigned to every family member, regardless of age—begging children don't come home unless they have something to bring to the family. And comparable realities exist in Cairo, Mumbai (Bombay), and many other urban centers.

One woman who found a way to survive at least temporarily was "Janet," and in her story sexual and family values collide with the need for economic survival. Janet lives in Manila. I met her very late at night in a bar in a poor working-class neighborhood. The bar has only a dirt floor, and sawhorses for seating at crude plank tables. It is darker inside than an American movie theater, except for a stage where a strobe light blinks crazily and Janet strips to raucous music. For this dance she is paid an extra U.S. $1.15 to supplement her $0.10 commission on each bottle of beer a patron buys for her. Short-term solutions for women so often involve selling what they have—their bodies. Only three of the fourteen girls working in this bar are on the dance schedule, and $1.15 is a fortune by most of their standards. But Janet, who is about seventeen and has been working in this bar for three years, doesn't want the extra cash tonight. She has sat for the last hour with me and my two companions on a sawhorse bench, crying because she can see no way to change her life. The owner gives her no choice about dancing tonight: dance or be fired.

My companions on the bench are part of a women's organization seeking to improve the working conditions of such girls and when possible to offer them alternative economic options. They have been coming to this and neighboring bars for months, buying enough drinks to keep the managers satisfied. But they still don't know "Janet's" real name or address. The world of these women and girls requires deception: of the more than three hundred prostituted women they have contacted, only three have given locatable names and addresses. These advocates work among the poorest of the poor, because their budget doesn't permit buying drinks in fancier bars, and because the financial alternatives they can suggest are so meager. For many women, short-term solutions become a longer-term cycle from which no escape can be found.[4]

And we must remember that women like Janet are living and working in the United States as well. Although we might prefer not to admit this reality, our country too has women who fall through the economic safety nets and see no option beyond selling their bodies.

## Ruth 3: Long-Term Planning

As we turn to chapter 3 of Ruth, we find Naomi speaking of Ruth's security for the longer term and devising a plan that involves acquiring a rich husband. As in Kamla's story, their hope is to escape the threat of starvation; as in Kamla's story, their plan is risky but the possibility of achieving greater economic security seems worth the risk. As we read Ruth's story today, knowing the ending, we can easily overlook the magnitude of her risk and view Kamla's situation as very different. Another true story from the Philippines will help to place the stories of Kamla and Janet in a larger context and draw the connecting thread between Kamla and Ruth.

A fourteen-year-old girl from a destitute family in a poor rural village was approached by a "recruiter" with an offer to work as a dancer in a wealthy foreign country (in the same way Mae Chan approached Kamla). She decided to accept the offer and told her woman pastor, who questioned her decision. The young girl used the book of Ruth to explain her action, saying, "Ruth put herself forward attractively to a rich man in hopes that he would marry her and take care of her family. I am doing the same. I hope a rich man from that country will choose me to marry and will look after me and my family. God made things turn out right for Ruth and God will take care of me too."

I do not know whether this fourteen-year-old understood that she would almost surely become not a dancer but a prostituted child, or whether she was excited or fearful about her proposed future far from home. Quite possibly her romanticized hope of a well-to-do husband blurred in her mind the boundary between dancing and the sexual activity that might be required of her in the course of meeting such a man. But I wondered how her use of Ruth came about. Did she think up this biblical rationale from the book of Ruth on her own (it seemed unlikely to me) or did someone plant it? Could that be the strategy of the recruiter? Could the child's own mother have suggested it or concurred with it? Did the girl really believe in the analogy, or was she seeking comfort wherever she could? What could her pastor finally reply? I do not know what this child finally did, but the number of prostituted children under age eighteen throughout the world is in the hundreds of thousands.

I have told the story of this Filipina child many times, in Asia and elsewhere, seeking women's responses to the question, "What do you think of this girl's interpretation of Ruth?" The first response, appropriately, has most often been silence. But after that, the women have regularly rejected the girl's use of Ruth, usually using one of these four explanations:

1. Some women cited the levirate law of Deuteronomy 25:5–10. The levirate law provided that when a man died without children, his brother should marry the widow and have a child by her to preserve the lineage of the man who had died. Ruth approached Boaz, according to this explanation, as a particular relative to whom the law gave a legal obligation to marry her. The women used their knowledge of this ancient biblical cultural custom to distinguish the intent of the biblical story from the interpretation of the Filipina child. Ruth's behavior was culturally appropriate, according to this view, and indeed this is a viewpoint found in many commentaries.

2. Other women adopted an interpretive strategy of cultural distance, simply insisting that Ruth's behavior might have been acceptable in ancient Israel, but it isn't now. Even women who knew nothing about ancient customs such as levirate marriage suggested this explanation. Again, it was assumed that Ruth did not engage in any questionable behavior.

3. Still others worked from a guideline that sex outside of marriage was wrong, so the girl must not accept the recruiter's offer; Ruth was irrelevant to the girl's situation.
4. Some looked to the biblical understanding of creation in the image of God as a basis for encouraging the child to honor her own body by refusing to go.

As heartfelt as these interpretations were, none could fully address the existential and practical question of the economic survival of that village family: How could they put sufficient rice on the table to remain alive?

As we think about this story and the efforts of women to achieve longer-term economic security for themselves and their families, we come up against the limits to the solidarity of action between Ruth and Naomi. While the story of Ruth and Naomi may be a model of women acting on their own, women making decisions, women taking initiative, and women cooperating with one another (in contrast here to Sarah and Hagar), these women lived within the overarching and undergirding context of a societal structure in which women's economic welfare was almost entirely dependent upon men. Then as now, such a world may be limiting and even threatening for women's welfare. Ruth in fact took a huge risk in approaching Boaz at night. His response, so far as we can discern it from the narrative, was ideal and honorable. But he might have made other choices: to have sex with her and then deny the relationship; or, to tell the whole village that she had inappropriately initiated contact with him in the night. Either of these actions would have been humiliating and ruinous to Ruth's already precarious future.

For women in a society such as Israel's, marriage (preferably to a well-off man) was the obvious and for the most part the only way to escape an economically marginalized life. For most women around the world, such a marriage is but a hope or a dream, a dream inculcated by cultural traditions everywhere, whether by parental expectations and planning, or by fairy tales such as Cinderella. The hope for marriage to a Prince Charming when paired with economic desperation leads girls to accept the false promises of slick (usually female) recruiters for the sex trade like Mae Chan in the story of Kamla. And yet, the question remains, as it does at the end of that story, "What is a girl like Kamla to do?" What are such girls in Manila or in New York to do? And recognizing that family values and economic survival do in fact collide in such a dehumanizing way, what is the responsibility of women who are comparatively well off to make a difference for the Kamlas of this world?

Where no rich or even marginally secure prospects for marriage are in immediate sight, desperately poor families turn to other strategies for survival. And of course the potential for tragedy is great. One of my most poignant visits was to a Taiwanese prison, essentially a detention camp, for foreign prostituted women who had been arrested, had served a mandatory three-month jail term, and were now awaiting repatriation to their home countries. But because the recruiters had smuggled them into Taiwan with forged papers, they had no proof of citizenship. According to my local hosts, the Taiwanese government was prepared to pay their airfare home, but their home countries refused to admit them (even when they spoke only the dialect of an obscure section of that country and could come from nowhere else). Some of these women had been detained for as long as two years. Some of them in fact were married and had husbands and children at home; they had sought domestic work overseas and had been forced into prostitution.

As we think about longer-term solutions, we realize that for women, the first answer in traditional cultures is usually marriage. When marriage will not provide economic stability, however meager, or a husband is not available, women turn to some form of employment to support themselves and their families. All too often, the seeming best or only option is to sell their bodies. And in many cases, they are tricked into doing that even when it is their intention to take other employment, such as domestic work. The story of Ruth has a "happy ending" within its own cultural context, as marriage, security, and a boy baby are the outcome of Ruth's initiative. But women cannot always realistically count on such an ending.

## Ruth 4: Marriage and Control of Property

In Ruth 4, the economic issue highlighted by the text is the relationship between marriage and land ownership. This is the focus of the complicated scene in which Boaz calls together the village elders at the gate to settle the matter of the redeemer, or next-of-kin. The narrative raises at least three puzzling issues that in my view we cannot resolve completely.

The first issue concerns Boaz's announcement that Naomi is selling a parcel of land belonging to her dead husband (4:3–4). While it is not unimaginable that Naomi had such a piece of land, why is it mentioned here so suddenly and so late in the story? Had it been cultivated? If so, why did its produce not belong to Naomi so that Ruth's gleaning would have been unnecessary? It seems safe to assume that the people who first heard or read this story would have understood the cultural system for property rights that would answer these questions, but modern commentators can only theorize about how that system worked. Whatever the system, it had not worked to Naomi's advantage up to this point of the story.

Second, why did Naomi not mention the nearer kinsmen earlier? This puzzle may be more easily understood in terms of the plot of the story: Boaz is the leading citizen of the village; the women seek to get him into a relationship with Ruth; and Boaz for his part is apparently attracted to Ruth. So the nearer kinsman plays the role of the last-moment obstacle to satisfactory resolution of the plot. He must be offered the chance to marry Ruth and then refuse his opportunity before the "happily ever after" ending of Boaz and Ruth's marriage is possible.

Third, why should the inheritance of the nearer kinsman be damaged by his redeeming of Naomi's land (4:6)? From a literary perspective, it appears that the nearer kinsman thinks up whatever excuse he can when he hears that he would also have to marry Ruth, who had the doubly undesirable background of being both previously married and also a Moabite. Thus Boaz appears all the more noble for doing what he wanted to do anyway.[5] Of course it is also possible that the nearer kinsman would have lost the land back to Naomi's husband's family if Ruth bore a son, and that situation would create an economic risk for him. He would have a larger family, but still no extra land.

Whatever the case about these details, it is clear that in the end Boaz acquires the parcel of land that belonged to Naomi's dead husband Elimelech and his sons (4:9), and he also acquires Ruth "to maintain the dead man's name on his inheritance" (4:10).

The complexity of the interconnection between land, a man's name, and women's economic status is illuminated by the story of the daughters of Zelophehad, recorded in Numbers 27 and 36. Five sisters whose father had died leaving no sons were permitted to inherit land so that their father's name would not be lost from the register of Israel. But they were then required to be married within their own clan, so that their father's name stayed connected to the land, and as soon as they married, the land would be handed over to their husbands. The story of these women illustrates the limitations to women's economic independence in Israel's agrarian culture. Even in the very exceptional case where daughters could inherit property, the inheritance was only temporary. The assumption was that such a woman would marry and that her property would be turned over to her husband and thus returned to male control. The idea of her own economic independence was beyond the imagining of the biblical narrators.[6]

The presumption that a married woman could not hold property (i.e., land) in her own right but was dependent upon her husband's economic status was apparently a basic feature of ancient Israelite society. It is difficult to ascertain more about women's economic condition from the scattered scraps of evidence we have from many different periods, but another indication of women's economic dependence upon men is found in the legislation concerning women's vows in Numbers 30. Vows were most likely paid as financial offerings to the sanctuary, and this legislation enabled the men to maintain control over family finances, as a father could always nullify vows made by his daughters and a husband could always nullify vows made by his wife, even any she had made before their marriage.[7]

The themes of land possession, inheritance, and economic control seem archaic at first glance; and to some degree the situation in Ruth is peculiar to an agrarian village context and not directly related to an industrialized and urbanized context typical of much of our world today. Nonetheless, questions of inheritance rights and the economic power of women remain significant in most cultures across the world. In 1991 a United Nations report summarized the legal rights of women in the world as follows:

> In much of the developing world, marriage and divorce laws supersede women's rights to own land, thus virtually disinheriting them. In Asia, the vast majority of women are landless as a result of discriminatory divorce and inheritance laws that do not give them access to land owned by men. In the Middle East, women are not legally autonomous individuals but need a male "guardian" to act for them in all legal transactions, including property acquisition and transfer, and applications for loans and credit. In 12 countries, the law does not allow women to seek employment, open a bank account or apply for a loan without the husband's authorization. Several Islamic countries have tried to modernize family law, but reforms had an impact only where an effort was made to inform women of their rights and provide them with legal counsel.[8]

While this global picture may seem remote from life in North America, where land and economic survival are not necessarily directly related, U.S. statistics concerning the poverty of women are grim. According to the U.S. Census Bureau year 2000 report, in 24.7 percent of households headed by females the family income fell below the poverty level, compared to only 4.7 percent of married couples.[9] These U.S. statistics deal with families with children and differ in that respect from the situation in Israelite culture and Naomi and Ruth's situation; and young women without children have employment options here that were not imaginable in Israel's context. Yet statistics also show that older single women in the United States (whether widowed, divorced, or never married) are more likely to be poor than are their male counterparts.[10]

In summary, the concluding chapter of Ruth reminds us of the context in which women's initiative for economic survival is set.

While individual circumstances may vary in different cultures and economies across the globe, it remains exceedingly difficult for women's independent initiative to succeed in those settings where men control most of the economic wealth.

The story of Ruth concludes with the traditional cultural ideal that problems of economic survival are eliminated by marriage to a rich and prominent man in the society. At the same time, I believe the story as a whole honors the ongoing struggle of women in every age for whom the ending of Ruth 4 never becomes a reality. Those women, who seek both short- and longer-term ways to feed their families in the absence of a wealthy male head of household, are represented both in Naomi's bitterness and despair and in Ruth's incredible daring. For those of us who do not find ourselves engaged in such a struggle for daily bread, the call of the book of Ruth, seen through women's eyes, may be this: to counter the necessity of a well-to-do husband by working in our own ways and in our own places toward a different social structure, one in which women's economic survival can be assured on other grounds.

## God's Role in the Story of Ruth

In the entire book of Ruth, only two actions are attributed directly to God. In 1:6 we read that "the LORD had considered his people and given them food," thus ending the famine in Bethlehem. And in 4:13 it is reported that the Lord made Ruth conceive. In the ancient Israelite worldview, these two events, human conception and the ending of famine, would indeed be the occurrences most especially viewed as beyond human control and attributed to divine intervention.

In the design of the story, these two direct interventions by God form a matched pair, a bracket within which the narrative is structured. The main part of the story is prefaced by the famine and the death of the male line without offspring, and God's interventions reverse these two opening negative events. The main action begins when Naomi receives word that the famine has ended, and Ruth's conception at the end of the story reverses the lack of descendants. Ruth's God-given conception may also highlight the contrast between her previous childlessness in ten years of marriage outside the land and her prompt conception when living in the land of promise. The twofold divine provision of food (fruit of the land) and offspring recalls God's promises to Abraham of land and many descendants (Gen. 13:14–16). And the recollection of those promises draws the reader's attention in turn to the lineage of Abraham and Sarah that continues through Ruth and Boaz to King David, who will rule over the land of promise.

Along with these two direct interventions by God, the story of Ruth includes numerous other references to the deity, all of them occurring in conversations between the various characters. Although no one addresses God directly, many of these conversational references function like prayers for God's blessing. The first is in Naomi's words of farewell blessing upon her daughters-in-law as she urges them to return home:

> "May the LORD deal kindly with you, as you have dealt with the dead and with me. The LORD grant that you may find security, each of you in the house of your husband." (1:8–9)

The NRSV expression "deal kindly with you" might also be translated "act faithfully or loyally toward you." In biblical tradition, invoking God's faithful action on behalf of another was done most often when the person invoking the blessing was unable to do anything further to change the situation. Naomi is unable to help Ruth and Orpah by providing them husbands, so she commits them and their need to God's faithful care. As Phyllis Trible points out, Naomi asks that God deal with them as they have dealt with her, setting the excellence of the Moabite women's faithfulness to their Israelite mother-in-law as a standard for divine kindness.[11]

In 1:21 Naomi speaks of God as she expresses her despair, reiterating the theme she expressed to her daughters-in-law in verse 13, when she said, "The hand of the LORD has turned against me." From the depths of her being Naomi pours out to the village women the pain of her experience:

"I went away full, but the LORD has brought me back empty;
why call me Naomi when the LORD has dealt harshly with
me, and the Almighty has brought calamity upon me?"

Although worded like direct interventions by God, these phrases
actually serve a different purpose, since they are interpretive
claims made by Naomi rather than "facts" in the sense of events
stated by the narrator of the story. Within the design of the narrative, Naomi's feeling that God has closed her future will be
changed by unfolding events. Indeed, God is already at work for
Naomi's future in the direct action of providing food that Ruth
will soon glean, but this is not yet in Naomi's perception.

Ruth 2:12 finds Boaz invoking a blessing upon Ruth, asking that
the God of Israel reward her for her deeds, that is, for her faithfulness to Naomi (v. 11). Boaz describes Ruth as having sought
refuge under God's wings, apparently an allusion to her travel to
the land of the God of Israel and her commitment to accept the
God of this new land and people as her own. Boaz's prayer for
Ruth's "full reward" by God joins Naomi's earlier prayer that "the
LORD deal kindly" with her. But as yet we do not see how these
prayers will be fulfilled.

In 2:20 we return to Naomi and again find her invoking a blessing and referring to kindness:

> Naomi said to her daughter-in-law, "Blessed be he by the
> LORD, whose kindness has not forsaken the living or the
> dead!"

The narrator has said that "as it happened, [Ruth] came to the
part of the field belonging to Boaz" (2:3). But through Naomi's
words in 2:20 we are shown that this turn of events was indeed no
happenstance. Rather, God was at work behind the scenes. In
reading the English of the NRSV, the referent of the phrase "whose
kindness has not forsaken the living or the dead" should properly
be the nearest antecedent, the Lord. The Hebrew of this verse,
however, offers two possible antecedents: the antecedent may be
the Lord or it may be "he," that is, Boaz. This ambiguity leads

the reader to imagine rightly that both Boaz and the Lord may have shown kindness. I believe the ambiguity is both deliberate and theologically profound. Through it we receive our first clue about how the previous indirect prayers of Naomi and Boaz for Ruth will receive an answer. God's action will not be direct intervention but will take shape through the actions of Boaz.

Naomi's exclamation in Ruth 2:20 represents a turning point for her from despair to hope, and hence from passivity to initiative. And it is indeed her initiative that will pave the way for Boaz's action. Thus both mother-in-law and kinsman bring to fruition through their actions the invocations of God's blessing they have made on Ruth's behalf. The call for blessing invites God to act, but the work that brings change is very much the work of faithful persons who act in accord with their words.

In 4:11 we find yet another invocation of blessing and prayer on behalf of Ruth:

> "May the LORD make the woman who is coming into your house like Rachel and Leah, who together built up the house of Israel."

Here the prayer is no longer for husband or for refuge, for these prayers have been fulfilled. The prayer is now for offspring, and for the carrying on of the family name in the village of Bethlehem. Spoken by the male elders to Boaz, it concerns male offspring, and Ruth is not even mentioned by name.[12] We are not able to avoid the traditional male orientation of the narrative here. And yet, it seems to me that Naomi's hope that her daughters-in-law would find new husbands (see her prayer blessing in 1:8–9) may have included the unexpressed hope that they would bear children as well. Security for a woman did not rest in marriage alone, but in marriage and children (as we have seen in the chapter on Sarah and Hagar). And so even within this male perspective in Ruth 4, the completion of the earlier prayers of Naomi may be envisioned in anticipation of the birth of a son.

Finally, in 4:14 the women of the community praise God, who has brought about the complete reversal of the desolation Naomi expressed in 1:13 and 1:21. Although the prayers of Naomi and Boaz on behalf of Ruth have been fulfilled, no one has prayed overtly for Naomi. But Ruth's loyalty to her from beginning to end has created conditions whereby Naomi's weeping is changed to rejoicing, and her sorrow to celebration.

Here indeed is a model for understanding God's ways with our lives and in our world. God's working is hidden and mysterious, like yeast at work in a loaf of bread, till all is transformed. To be sure, from time to time there may be some change in life that we attribute only to the intervention of God, but more often God is at work through the everyday actions of faithful people seeking to manifest divine loyalty in their interactions with those around them. I find this theme from the narrative of Ruth well expressed in one of my favorite new hymns, which I learned in Asia:

> He came singing love and He lived singing love;
> He died, singing love.
> He arose in silence.
> For the love to go on we must make it our song;
> You and I be the singers.[13]
> (The verse repeats three times, substituting the words "faith,"
>     "hope," and "peace" for "love.")

As we work to change social structures so that women's survival is not so precarious, God is at work in us.

### Questions for Personal Reflection or Group Study

1.  Some women admire Ruth's devotion to Naomi and seek to emulate it, while others find that Ruth's devotion models a level of responsibility that can be oppressive or unhealthy. What is your own reaction?
2.  How in your experience have differences in culture, ethnicity, or religion affected the relationship between mothers-in-law and daughters-in-law or other family members (your own or those of people you know)?

3. Ruth was a foreigner from the hated Moabite group, yet she became an ancestor of King David and is mentioned in Matthew's genealogy of Jesus. What does her story suggest to you about relationships across ethnic or national boundaries? How may her story inform your response to issues of diversity and immigration generally and in your own community?
4. Have there been times in your life when you have felt God intervened directly in circumstances? How have you experienced God working through the lives of other people? In what ways do you sense that God may be using you to make a difference in the world?
5. Prostitution, including child prostitution, is an organized international business, not just a matter of isolated individuals. If you are not familiar with this problem, or would like to learn more, spend some time in your local library, inquire from your denominational church office, or check the Internet.
6. In many parts of the world grassroots women's organizations are seeking ways to help women gain greater financial security. Often churches or other religious groups are sponsoring such projects. Are there nongovernment groups or programs like this in your community? If not, can one be started? What can you individually commit yourself to do toward reducing poverty among women?

## Notes

1. For more about this focus and for a study that develops other themes in the story of Ruth, see Katharine Doob Sakenfeld, *Ruth* (Interpretation Commentary Series; Louisville, Ky.: Westminster John Knox Press, 1999).
2. Foundation for Women, *Kamla*, 2nd ed., English trans. Ananya Ungphakorn (Bangkok, Thailand: Foundation for Women, 1990).
3. The term "prostituted woman/child" is preferred by many antiprostitution advocates over the more familiar "prostitute." The newer expression avoids labeling and defining the person only by her activity, and it also indicates the complicity both of the individual sexual partners and of the complex sex-trade economic structures in the life of the prostituted person.

4.  See Katharine Doob Sakenfeld, "'Feminist' Theology and Biblical Interpretation," in *Biblical Theology: Problems and Perspectives* (ed. Steven J. Kraftchick, Charles D. Myers Jr., and Ben C. Ollenburger; Nashville: Abingdon Press, 1995), 256.

5.  Danna Nolan Fewell and David Miller Gunn, *Compromising Redemption: Relating Characters in the Book of Ruth* (Louisville, Ky.: Westminster John Knox Press, 1990), 59–61.

6.  For a fuller discussion of Num. 27 and 36, see Katharine Doob Sakenfeld, "Feminist Biblical Interpretation," *Theology Today* 46, no. 2 (1989): 154–68.

7.  For more detail, see Katharine Doob Sakenfeld, *Journeying with God: A Commentary on the Book of Numbers* (Grand Rapids: Eerdmans, 1995), 160–64.

8.  *Women: Challenges to the Year 2000* (New York: United Nations, 1991), 11.

9.  Joseph Dalaker, U.S. Census Bureau, Current Population Reports, Series P60–214, *Poverty in the United States: 2000*, U.S. Government Printing Office, Washington, D.C., 2001, 2, Table A. <http://www.census.gov/prod/2001pubs/p60-214.pdf>

    > The Census Bureau uses a set of money income thresholds that vary by family size and composition to determine who is poor. If a family's total income is less than that family's threshold, then that family, and every individual in it, is considered poor. The official poverty thresholds do not vary geographically, but they are updated annually for inflation using the Consumer Price Index (CPI-U). The official poverty definition counts money income before taxes and does not include capital gains and noncash benefits (such as public housing, Medicaid, and food stamps). (*Poverty in the United States: 2000*, 5.)

10. For instance, according to a 1998 government report, "Women and Retirement Security," in 1997 the overall poverty rate for women age 65 and over was 13.1 percent compared with 7.0 percent for men. Poverty rates for widows (18.0 percent), divorced women (22.2 percent), and women never married (20.0 percent) were higher. See National Economic Council Interagency Working Group on Social Security, "Women and Retirement Security," 5. <http://www.ssa.gov/policy/pubs/sswomen.pdf>

11. Phyllis Trible, *God and the Rhetoric of Sexuality* (Philadelphia: Fortress Press, 1978), 169–70.

12. Ibid., 191.

13. Christian Conference of Asia and Asian Institute for Liturgy and Music, *Sound the Bamboo: C.C.A. Hymnal 1990* (Manila, Philippines: Asian Institute for Liturgy and Music, 1990), song 205. Used by permission.

# Chapter Three

# Vashti and Esther: Models of Resistance
## Esther 1–10

In this chapter we turn to a study of Vashti and Esther, two women whom the biblical story describes as successive queens of the great Persian Empire. The book begins with the brief but exceedingly important story of Vashti and why she lost her crown. The rest of the book then focuses on Esther's story; it is a traditional tale of intrigue involving Jews in a foreign royal household, like the story of Abraham in the court of the Egyptian Pharaoh (Gen. 12) or Daniel in the court of Babylon (Dan. 1–6). Although the king in the Esther narrative is known from other sources, we cannot be sure about the other characters, and scholars disagree about how much of the story actually took place as described. Whatever the background of the story, it is surely based in Jewish experience of fear and persecution in Persian times.

Vashti and Esther remind us that even amidst great married wealth and royal status there remain many problems for women to confront. Life for them in the lavish Persian court could hardly have been more different from the lives and struggles of the tent-dwelling Sarah and Hagar or Ruth and Naomi in the village of Bethlehem. And while the royal court setting is just as remote from most of our own circumstances as a tent or an agrarian subsistence village, here too we will find and recognize women whose challenges and decisions are related to those we all must face today. Esther and Vashti represent two different models of resistance to the misuse of power and authority. One says an emphatic "No!"; the other works within the structures of the system to achieve her goal. As we look at their stories, we will focus on their two ways of working in a male-dominated context.

## The Biblical Story

The following summary is quite brief, as I recount parts of the story in greater detail in the course of the chapter. Here is a chance for you to get oriented to the outline and the names of the major characters of the narrative.

The powerful King Ahasuerus ruled an empire stretching "from India to Ethiopia" (Esth. 1:1). During a men-only banquet for the leaders of his kingdom, he summoned his wife Vashti to appear before the assembled guests. Vashti refused, and was deposed. A lengthy search was instituted for a new queen, and many young women were brought to the palace, among them Esther (also called Hadassah), a Jewish orphan who had been brought up by her older cousin Mordecai. After rejecting many women, the king selected Esther as the new queen. A short while later, Mordecai (who lived near the palace) discovered and reported to Esther a plot against the king. The king's life was saved, and Mordecai's name and the event were recorded in the royal annals.

Five years passed, and Haman, the king's top official, became angry at Mordecai for refusing to obey a royal edict to bow before him. In retaliation, Haman devised a plan to kill not just the Jew Mordecai, but all the Jews of the empire. To achieve this goal Haman promulgated a royal decree authorizing the slaughter of all Jews on a specified day. Esther learned of the plan from Mordecai, who asked her to intercede with the king. She did this through a carefully orchestrated series of events that resulted both in Haman's downfall and death on the very gallows he had built for Mordecai and in Mordecai's appointment as Haman's replacement. Esther and Mordecai arranged for a royal decree that authorized the Jews of the empire to defend themselves on the day marked for their extermination. On the appointed date, the Jews killed thousands of their enemies in the capital city and throughout the empire. The Jews celebrated the failure of Haman's plot, and the story is still celebrated today at the annual Jewish festival called Purim.

## Self-Defense or Excessive Force?

Before discussing Vashti or Esther, it is important to confront the difficult and troubling issue that arises at the end of the book of Esther: the killing of their enemies by the Jews. The issue is the treatment of enemies, and Esther's central role reminds us that women as well as men may support violence and killing. I raise this issue at the beginning of the chapter because many readers find it so disturbing. It cannot be ignored, yet it should not prevent us from appreciating other parts of the story.

Although the story centers on Esther's effort to resist the planned extermination of the Jewish population of Persia, this goal is not accomplished by simply canceling Haman's decree (probably because according to tradition royal Persian decrees were irrevocable). Instead a new decree is sent out that will permit the Jews to "defend their lives, to destroy, to kill, and to annihilate any armed force of any people or province that might attack them" (8:11). Although this phrasing of the decree is defensive, it empowers the Jews and terrifies their enemies (9:2–3), with cause as it turns out, for on the appointed day,

> the Jews struck down all their enemies with the sword, slaughtering and destroying them, and did as they pleased to those who hated them (9:5).

Here we find no mention that the Jews were defending themselves from an enemy's attack, and when the number killed that day in the capital city was reported to the king, Esther requested that the killing be permitted to continue for a second day (9:13–15).

Because of this ending, the book of Esther has not been much liked by many commentators in Jewish as well as in Christian circles. A number of scholars[1] believe that the book originally ended with chapter 8, thus keeping the decree permitting self-defense but eliminating the story of the Jewish initiative in the slaughter. But a hypothesis about an unknown earlier edition of the book does not solve the problem presented by the current form of the story handed down in Jewish and Christian Scripture.

In presenting the story of Esther, I do not intend to justify either the seemingly disproportional slaughter at the end of the story or Esther's part in it. This killing of enemies is difficult for many of us to accept, and with reason. Yet we need to remember that uprisings against genocidal regimes are hardly unusual, and that, depending on who is rebelling, we sometimes praise the insurgents for heroic action. Moreover, different people have quite different views of who is an oppressor, who is a victim, and the action needed to create greater safety for those who are threatened. We should also keep in mind the centuries-long history of pogroms against Jews during which they had no Queen Esther, no one who had any power to prevent their slaughter or authorize any defense or retaliation. The horrors of the Holocaust are but the last in a long series of such events—events that were perpetrated not by ancient Persians, but by Christians in the name of Jesus.

Before we criticize the conclusion of the book of Esther too harshly, let us remember how difficult it is in our own time to distinguish between preemptive defensive strikes and uncalled-for aggression, between actions based in revenge and those based in legitimate fear for personal and communal safety. And let us also remember that contemporary situations calling for such distinctions are not limited to the Middle East, but can be found among many peoples in far-flung areas of the globe ranging from Rwanda and the Congo to Kashmir, to Eastern Europe, and even to the United States itself, especially since 9/11.

### Queen Esther

And so we turn to Esther, whose story has many complex twists and turns. We'll come back to Vashti later.

King Ahasuerus needs a new queen. Beautiful maidens from across the land are brought to the court, given a year of beauty treatments, then sent one by one to the king's bed. After one night with the king, each young woman is returned to a different section of the harem and does not go again to the king unless summoned by name. Esther, who keeps secret her Jewish identity, is among those in the harem.

Esther's turn comes (four years after the beginning of this program to identify a new queen—imagine the number of virgins the king has deflowered in the meantime!)—and she immediately wins the king's affection. He sets a royal crown on her head, proclaims her queen, gives a big party, and grants a national holiday.

When Haman develops his plan to destroy all the Jews, he is careful not to disclose to King Ahasuerus that he is targeting the Jews. He simply tells the king that "a certain people . . . do not keep the king's laws" (3:8) and offers a huge sum of money for the royal treasury if the king agrees to let Haman issue a decree for their destruction. Ahasuerus does not ask any questions about the identity of this "certain people," or about the accuracy of Haman's accusation; he just authorizes Haman to carry out his plan. When the decree is promulgated throughout the empire, Mordecai (who seems to have some minor position on the outskirts of the palace) hears about it although Esther within the king's court does not.

Mordecai and the other Jews lament the decree in sackcloth and ashes and Mordecai urges Esther to plead before the king on behalf of the Jews. Esther hesitates, unsure, for entering the king's presence unbidden was cause to be put to death, unless he himself granted an exception. But she is convinced of the need to act by Mordecai's powerful words:

> Do not think that in the king's palace you will escape any more than all the other Jews. For if you keep silence at such a time as this, relief and deliverance will rise for the Jews from another quarter, but you and your father's family will perish. Who knows? Perhaps you have come to royal dignity for just such a time as this. (4:13–14)

Esther asks that all the Jews in the capital city of Susa join her and her attendants in a three-day fast, after which she will approach the king, "though it is against the law; and if I perish, I perish" (4:16).

Before continuing with the story, it will be helpful to explain that there are actually three different versions of the book of Esther. One is in Hebrew; and this is the one that appears in Jewish Scripture and in most Protestant Bibles. There are also two different versions in Greek. These two Greek versions between them include six extended passages with a total of 107 verses that are not in the Hebrew version. You may or may not find these six additions in your Bible. Some Protestant Bibles have only the translation of the Hebrew version. In other Protestant Bibles, the six passages, called "Additions to Esther," are in a separate section known as the Apocrypha.[2] In Roman Catholic and some ecumenical Bibles, the six additions from the Greek are inserted at the appropriate points into the basic narrative.

Each of the three versions is a bit different from the others, and the details about Esther vary, even as the overall contours of the story remain similar.[3] The most notable difference is that the Greek versions contain many references to God, who is not mentioned at all in the Hebrew version. The Greek also includes a long prayer that Esther utters during her three days of fasting. In this prayer, she pleads:

> O Lord, do not surrender your scepter to what has no being; and do not let them laugh at our downfall; but turn their plan against them, and make an example of him who began this against us. Remember, O Lord; make yourself known in this time of our affliction, and give me courage, O King of the gods and Master of all dominion! Put eloquent speech in my mouth before the lion, and turn his heart to hate the man who is fighting against us, so that there may be an end of him and those who agree with him. But save us by your hand, and help me, who am alone and have no helper but you, O Lord. (Add. Esth. 14:11–14)

Esther also indicates in the prayer that she hates her position as queen, abhors sharing the king's bed, avoids wearing her crown unless forced to do so, and has had no joy since the day that I was brought here until now, except in you, O Lord God of Abraham. O God, whose might is over all, hear the voice of the despairing, and save us from the hands of evildoers. And save me from my fear! (Add. Esth. 14:18–19)

Esther approaches the king, who immediately holds out his golden scepter so that she is safe. Despite his encouragement, however, Esther asks not for what she really wants, but only that the king and Haman attend a private banquet she will prepare for them. At the banquet, the king again offers her whatever she desires, but she asks only that he and Haman attend a second banquet.

In the interlude between the two banquets, Haman, still frustrated by Mordecai's refusal to do obeisance, has a gallows built and plans to convince the king to hang the insolent Jew. But that same night the king, reading the book of royal annals, recalls that Mordecai had saved his life and learns that he was never rewarded. The next morning, the king asks Haman how he should treat one whom he wishes to honor. Haman, thinking of course that the king wants to honor him, proposes elaborate ceremonies; to his chagrin, he is then required personally to lavish all those ceremonies upon the hated Mordecai.

Soon Esther's second private banquet gets under way, again with the king and Haman as her guests, and now Esther reveals her Jewish heritage and expresses her wish that she and her people be saved from the person who has plotted against them. The dramatic climax deserves to be quoted at length:

> Then King Ahasuerus said to Queen Esther, "Who is he, and where is he, who has presumed to do this?" Esther said, "A foe and enemy, this wicked Haman!" Then Haman was terrified before the king and the queen. The king rose from the feast in wrath and went into the palace garden, but Haman stayed to beg his life from Queen Esther, for he saw that the king had determined to destroy him. When the king

returned from the palace garden to the banquet hall, Haman had thrown himself on the couch where Esther was reclining; and the king said, "Will he even assault the queen in my presence, in my own house?" . . . So they hanged Haman on the gallows that he had prepared for Mordecai. Then the anger of the king abated.

On that day King Ahasuerus gave to Queen Esther the house of Haman, the enemy of the Jews; and Mordecai came before the king, for Esther had told what he was to her. Then the king took off his signet ring, which he had taken from Haman, and gave it to Mordecai. (Esth. 7:5–8a, 10; 8:1–2a)

But the rescue thus far is only personal for Esther and Mordecai, as Haman's decree has not been rescinded. In the next chapter, Esther again approaches the king and he allows her and Mordecai to prepare their own edict in the king's name. That edict, as I discussed above, allows the Jews to annihilate any attackers on the day originally decreed for Haman's pogrom. So "there was gladness and joy among the Jews, a festival and a holiday" (8:17).

### Beauty Conquers All?

What should we make of this biblical story, in which God is not even mentioned in the Hebrew version and thus is much further behind the scene than in the other stories we have considered? Esther is a controversial figure. Male and female scholars alike are divided over her portrayal in this book. Some scholars have seen the main protagonist not as Esther but as Mordecai, since he sends her instructions and eventually receives the king's signet ring. Others have focused on Esther's physical appearance as her principal asset. One writes, for example, that "Esther is the stereotypical woman in a man's world. She wins favor by the physical beauty of her appearance, and then by her ability to satisfy sexually."[4]

Sidnie White is among those women scholars who have most directly challenged this negative assessment of Esther. It is certainly true that Esther was beautiful. The text makes that explicit

(2:7). But White points out that in the harem Esther "won" favor with the man in charge of the harem (2:9). The Hebrew verb chosen by the narrator indicates that the favor was the result of Esther's action, rather than being passively acquired.[5]

It is also true that "Esther had not revealed her kindred or her people, as Mordecai had charged her; for Esther obeyed Mordecai just as when she was brought up by him" (2:20). Does her obedience mean that she unthinkingly followed his advice, just because she had always done so? It seems more likely that we have a picture of a young woman who, thrust into an unfamiliar context, carefully follows the suggestion of a guardian whose counsel has proved trustworthy in the past. Following Mordecai's advice should hardly be counted as a lack of intelligence or initiative on Esther's part. Moreover, as White points out, Esther's secret is necessary to the plot; the story line would collapse if her Jewish heritage were known from the outset.[6]

From our modern perspective, we can certainly feel ambivalence, if not outright discomfort and disagreement, with Esther's enhancing her beauty and using her sexual allure to gain the king's favor when her opportunity arises. In our time and our culture, many people say that it is inappropriate for women to use their physical appearance or so-called "feminine wiles" to gain special privilege over fellow employees in the workplace.

And yet we know that not everyone agrees, and that even what people say is not always what they really believe, or what actually happens. In some job settings, some women do use their physical appearance deliberately to gain advantage, and some men either do not object or do not recognize that reality. Women who try to make sure that those in authority concentrate on their work performance rather than their appearance may be criticized for not making the most of their physical appearance. And male or female peers may think that women who do gain advancement have succeeded because of factors related to their sexuality or appearance, whether or not this is actually the case. The reality of harassment in the workplace, where peers or superiors do in fact try to take advantage of sexual difference, further complicates our perspective on Esther's circumstances.

It is a challenge to find a satisfactory balance between attention to professional performance and to personal appearance, whether for ourselves or for those around us. Some time ago, while visiting in a European country, I heard an excellent woman preacher. Even as I listened to her, I found myself thinking that her hairstyle was just awful. Later I was told that her parishioners were not appreciative of her gifts, even though other, male, pastors in the area were quite supportive. And I found myself wondering silently whether a new hairstyle would make a difference in how people thought of her. In retrospect I was shocked at myself: I did not know this pastor, I could barely speak her native language, I did not hear her in her own parish setting, I knew next to nothing of the hairstyles being worn in her context. We hope to concentrate on the work people accomplish, yet inevitably other factors make their way into our assessments. It is often not easy to sort out the relationship between what we do and how we look.

In contrast to our own situation, in Esther's ancient cultural context her options were limited or nonexistent. Esther was part of a roundup of beautiful girls; she did not volunteer for the harem. Once she was there, she had a choice. She could resist her situation, and be assured of meeting the fate of all the others, who were sent off to the second section of the harem after deflowering by the king, to live there for the rest of their lives unless the king happened to remember their name and call them back for another night (2:14). Or, she could act in a way that would "win favor" in the palace and thus have a possibility of becoming the new queen.

Actually the text does not tell us anything about what Esther was thinking or indicate that she made a conscious choice. We are just told that she "won favor" with the man in charge of the harem, who then gave her special consideration that she did not refuse. We can make ethical arguments in favor of each option that we imagine Esther might have had, but the point is that we should not automatically despise her apparent choice to act in a pleasing manner and take advantage of the food and cosmetics made available to her. As it turns out, the power that came to Esther as a result of her actions was invaluable to her people.

Mordecai's donning of sackcloth and ashes in response to Haman's edict was perhaps a simple sign of mourning, as was typical in Old Testament times. He may also have hoped to evoke a saving response from the God who is not mentioned in the text. But in a story written to describe events in which there is no divine intervention, it is Esther's action, not sackcloth and ashes, that makes the difference in the survival of the Jews.

By the time of Haman's decree, Esther had been queen for five years; yet her initially hesitant response to Mordecai's plea shows that she could not be confident of the king's attitude toward her. Nonetheless she decided to take action and approached the king. Why did she use the circuitous route of two private banquets on the way to expressing her real request? After all, when she entered the king's chamber he immediately said she could have whatever she wanted. Perhaps she was afraid; after all, she wanted to challenge a decree promulgated by the king's most senior adviser, a decree that had resulted in large sums given to the treasury. A favorable response from King Ahasuerus, who was infamous in the ancient world for his sharp temper, could not be assured.

Even if Esther was afraid, however, that does not mean that fear was the driving force behind her delaying tactics. Perhaps rather than simply avoiding the inevitable moment when she must state her real request, she was laying strategic groundwork to ensure a successful appeal. Holding a second banquet accomplished two things: First, it furthered Haman's false sense of security. Second, it put the king in a position where he was even more likely to acquiesce to her risky request. When he committed himself at the first banquet to give her whatever she wanted, she asked him to attend the second banquet and promised to tell him her request at that time. By agreeing to attend, the king was more committed to granting her petition.[7] Surely with this strategy Esther was using her own wisdom, not just her beauty, and not instructions from Mordecai.

When she finally revealed her request, she asked first for her own life, then for the life of her people, beginning with what she knew the king valued, and then expanding her request. Arguing for the severity of the situation, she explained that she would have remained silent if the Jews had only been sold into slavery, but the command to put them to death would be disadvantageous to the king and his realm. In response, the king directed his rage at Haman. Even so, once Haman was dead on his own gallows and Mordecai had been given his place of authority, Haman's edict remained in place—only Esther and Mordecai had been saved.

So Esther again risked approaching the king unbidden, and again he extended his scepter. We are reminded by the repetition of that sequence that one success did not ensure another. Each time Esther's risk was new. In this visit, she appealed again to the king's personal feeling for her (8:6):

> "How can I bear to see the calamity that is coming on my people? Or how can I bear to see the destruction of my kindred?" (8:6)

She also capitalized on the king's apparent desire to please her by connecting it to his presumed desire to do right:

> "If it pleases the king, and if I have won his favor, and if the thing seems right before the king, and I have his approval, let an order be written to revoke the letters devised by Haman." (8:5)

In response, the king gave his permission to Esther to "write as you please with regard to the Jews, in the name of the king" (8:8).

Can Esther serve as a model for women in our own time who are seeking change? I have already indicated some of the difficulties and ambivalence about Esther's character in this story. It is true that Esther's acquiescence in the use of beauty to gain access to power sets an example that many women wish to oppose as a general principle. But as in all of life, general principles and specific situations do not always mesh neatly. We might imagine that Esther could have refused to cooperate in the harem, thus making a personal statement that would presumably have been unheard, unseen, and unnoticed except perhaps by other girls in the harem. There might have been a benefit to others, but we have no secure basis for speculation about a path Esther did not choose. It seems unlikely that she would have been in a position to challenge Haman's decree. Of course Esther did not know at the start that she might be able to use a position of power to save her people. But when she did find herself faced with such a challenge, she acted wisely and successfully.

We should also remember that even as queen, Esther's power was limited. The king had the right to put her to death for an unauthorized appearance, as was the rule for any member of the court. The risk that she took in approaching the king should be as much a part of what we remember about her story as the beauty contest by which she became queen.

African-American poet Audre Lorde has asked whether the master's tools can be effective in dismantling the master's house.[8] Her essay raises the important question of whether or not any system can be fundamentally transformed from the inside. One may ask, for example, whether women should seek to join a traditional hierarchy such as the U.S. Senate, or the Roman Catholic clergy or the Protestant clergy in order to try to change the institution. By joining have they already sold out to the system, so that change remains impossible? Our systems may not be dependent on beauty to function, but Esther's was, and she worked within the system available to her. Today women and men stand on both sides of that debate. And so, it turns out, do the two women in the book of Esther.

## Queen Vashti

Vashti has been more popular among feminist writers than Esther, generally under the rubric, "And She Said 'No!'" The story of Vashti in chapter 1 opens with a banquet scene that makes all others in the Bible seem trivial and boring by comparison. For 180 days (six months!) the king displayed his splendor and pomp for officials, ministers, army, nobles, and provincial governors. To conclude the festivities, he put on a seven-day banquet in his palace, which was filled with linen hangings, marble columns, mosaic floors, silver and gold couches, and gold drinking goblets. At the banquet the guests drank "by flagons, without restraint" (1:8). This banquet was for men only; Queen Vashti was giving a concurrent women's banquet in another section of the palace.

On the seventh day the drunken king ordered his attendants "to bring Queen Vashti before the king, wearing the royal crown, in order to show the peoples and the officials her beauty; for she was fair to behold. But Queen Vashti refused to come at the king's command" (1:11–12).

We are not told what motivated Vashti's unexpected "No" to the command conveyed by the king's attendants. To many readers, her refusal to display herself before a roomful of drunken men suggests personal reserve and integrity. Some traditions suggest that the requirement that she wear her crown implies that she was commanded to wear the crown but nothing else, thus appearing naked, although the text does not specify this. Whether Vashti refused out of modesty or for some other reason, it made no difference to the king.

Ahasuerus became enraged, for no one disobeys the king, least of all his wife, and particularly not in the presence of hundreds of guests before whom the king may now be a laughingstock. So he consulted his legal advisers, asking, "What is to be done to Queen Vashti because she has not performed the command of King Ahasuerus?" (1:15). The chief adviser, Memucan, gave this reply:

> Not only has Queen Vashti done wrong to the king, but also to all the officials and all the peoples who are in all the provinces of King Ahasuerus. For this deed of the queen will be made known to all women, causing them to look with contempt on their husbands, since they will say, "King Ahasuerus commanded Queen Vashti to be brought before him, and she did not come." This very day the noble ladies of Persia and Media who have heard of the queen's behavior will rebel against the king's officials, and there will be no end of contempt and wrath! If it pleases the king, let a royal order go out from him, and let it be written among the laws of the Persians and the Medes so that it may not be altered, that

Vashti is never again to come before King Ahasuerus; and let the king give her royal position to another who is better than she. So when the decree made by the king is proclaimed throughout all his kingdom, vast as it is, all women will give honor to their husbands, high and low alike. (1:16–20)

King Ahasuerus was infamous for his emotional volatility, especially on the side of rage at what displeased him. No wonder Esther would later worry, knowing of his reaction to Vashti's behavior. But in chapter 1 the king's rage had consequences that led far beyond Vashti. Fear that Vashti's behavior would become an example to other leading women and that social chaos would result (or, at least, chaos from the men's point of view) led to a decree of Vashti's banishment, and letters were sent forth to all corners of the kingdom declaring that "every man should be master in his own house" (1:22). As if that could be accomplished by decree! If it could have been, Vashti would never have said, "No!"

As we recognize that no decree can really prevent the existence of women like Vashti, we are invited at one level to laugh at the desperately frightened male leadership of the empire. And in the best of worlds, this story can be read as satire, poking fun at the king. After all, the successor queen cooperates and does not say "No," but she still gets her own way by other means. The king does not finally rule his kingdom apart from her desires.

Yet it is hard for me to enjoy this underlying humor, for Vashti's story has too much ancient and contemporary truth for comfort. Whatever the issue, whether it is women or men who are in the forefront, it seems that the greater the publicity the greater the potential for backlash. Publicly recognized dissenters are often treated harshly in an effort to warn others to toe the line. Stories of brave resistance have great power to influence and transform others. But the threat of severe reprisal, wielded with the intention of increasing people's fear, is a powerful weapon available to those in authority seeking to hold on to their power. In the church, the threat of excommunication or defrocking can silence dissent; in the public sector, the threat may be the loss of one's job, demotion, humiliation. In the relative privacy of the family, the threat may be physical or verbal abuse, financial pressure, or fear of embarrassment. Yet many do overcome their fear, and their "No," despite accompanying pain, may make a positive difference for themselves and sometimes for others as well.

There are many contemporary examples of persons who have said, "No!" Women have left abusive marriages, even at great cost; women have objected to harassment in the workplace; myriad African-Americans continue to say "No" to systemic racism; whistle-blowers have exposed cases of corporate or governmental fraud or mismanagement. Some who have said "No" are well known, but most are unheralded persons, perhaps known only to a local newspaper, perhaps not even that, who have taken their stand for human dignity. Vashti's "No!" is a model for women and men alike.

## Models of Resistance

The book of Esther presents us with two models of resistance to wrong: Vashti exercised personal direct dissent that led to her banishment and efforts at further societal repression; Esther worked "within the system," even using feminine wiles, as a strategy for saving herself and others. What happens if we put Esther and Vashti into dialogue, one woman who refuses to come when commanded to do so, the other who dares to appear without being called for?[9] Carol Lakey Hess has done just that, using the stories of Esther and Vashti as framing images for her study of women's development. She notes:

> We need not pit Vashti and Esther against one another. Those who seek to shape the course of history are not of one mold. Vashti, although clearly cooperative on many matters (such as being a beautiful and gracious host for the women's banquet), comes to a point of uncompromising insistence on what she sees as right. Esther, after a history of compliance . . . reaches a point where she throws role expectations to the winds. Though she was successful, that success was not predictable.[10]

Hess then plays imaginatively with the story, in the style of the Jewish tradition of "making midrash," a tradition of expanding stories in a way that explores their contemporary relevance. Hess imagines that the banished Vashti lives in hiding in an outlying district, her whereabouts known to a select few who remain in the royal court. When Esther faces the crisis of Haman's decree, she arranges, at obvious risk to herself, to be taken to Vashti. Esther acknowledges Vashti as queen, speaks in admiration of what Vashti did, and then seeks Vashti's advice on how to save her people from Haman's edict. Vashti reflects:

> "If I were to do everything over, I would do the same thing that I did before. I would stand up and tell the king what I thought."
>
> "Yes, your majesty, I know," replied the young queen [Esther] with a hint of shame. "But, pray do not be angry, I am indebted to you but I am not you."
>
> "No you are not me and my way is not the only way." [11]

In Hess's midrash, Esther's strategy for winning over the king is proposed by Vashti:

> "The King wants beauty and submission . . . give him what he wants. Dress up in your finest! Perfume yourself exquisitely! Prepare a sumptuous banquet!"

The two queens then work together to devise the plan carried out by Esther.[12] In Hess's midrash Esther's plan is no longer her private plan, but one worked out with Vashti, each woman respecting the style of the other and the particular circumstances that require a response toward fuller humanity of women and all people.

Hess's midrash conveys a powerful message. As we seek to promote justice, mercy, and peace, we must not think that tactics do not matter; at the same time we must not become bogged down in infighting about the "best" way to challenge and change the rulers and powers of this world. Over the long haul, a variety of approaches to challenging the status quo will be needed. As we work together, whether like Vashti saying "No!" or like Esther within the structures in which we find ourselves, we may all be encouraged by joining in phrases from Esther's prayer:

> O Lord, do not surrender your scepter to what has no being; and do not let them laugh at our downfall; but turn their plan against them. . . . Remember, O Lord; make yourself known in this time of our affliction, and give me courage. . . . Put eloquent speech in my mouth before the lion. . . . Save us by your hand. . . . O God, whose might is over all, hear the voice of the despairing, and save us from the hands of evildoers. And save me from my fear! (Add. Esth. 14:11–19)

## Questions for Individual Reflection or Group Study

1. In your experience, have there been times when physical appearance has made a difference in women's effectiveness or success in the workplace? In what ways? Do you think it should make a difference? Why or why not? Under what circumstances?

2. Do you think of yourself as more like Esther (working within the system) or more like Vashti (standing against systems you disapprove of)? To what extent does your approach depend on the specific issue or circumstances?

3. Can you think of occasions when you have worked with someone whose strategy for dealing with an unjust situation is very different from your own? How have you handled your disagreements?

4. Does the violent ending of the story in chapter 9 affect your ability to relate to Esther? If yes, why and in what way? If no, why?

5. In what ways do you find it possible to consider experiences of royalty like Esther's and Vashti's as instructive for the lives of ordinary women? Are there gaps between their life situation and yours that make it difficult to connect with them? How do these gaps compare to those between you and Ruth or Hagar (see previous chapters)?

6. What issue of human justice is most on your heart at this time? How can Vashti or Esther's stories encourage or empower you with regard to that issue?
7. In one version of the book of Esther, God's name does not appear; another version contains lengthy prayers to God. In your experience, what happens when "secular" people who focus their lives on human action and "religious" people who have a deep faith in God and pray regularly work together for the same cause?

## Notes

1. For example, David J. A. Clines, *The Esther Scroll: The Story of the Story* (Journal for the Study of the Old Testament Supplement Series 30; Sheffield: JSOT Press, 1984), 34–49; Sidnie Ann White, "Esther: A Feminine Model for Jewish Diaspora," in *Gender and Difference in Ancient Israel* (ed. Peggy L. Day; Minneapolis: Fortress Press, 1989), 164.
2. The Apocrypha contains a number of additional Old Testament writings that are known only in the Greek language, not Hebrew, and thus have been called deuterocanonical, meaning they are of secondary status in the canon. The church has debated their canonical status from earliest times. Today they are recognized as canonical by the Catholic and Orthodox traditions, but not by Protestant communities.
3. A quite technical scholarly description of these differences has been prepared by Linda Day. See Linda Day, *Three Faces of a Queen: Characterization in the Books of Esther* (Sheffield: Sheffield Academic Press, 1995).
4. Alice Laffey, *An Introduction to the Old Testament: A Feminist Perspective* (Philadelphia: Fortress Press, 1988), 216.
5. White, "Esther," 167.
6. Ibid., 167–68.
7. See Clines, *Esther Scroll*, 144.
8. Audre Lorde, "The Master's Tools Will Never Dismantle the Master's House," in *Sister Outsider: Essays and Speeches* (Trumansburg, N.Y.: Crossing Press, 1984), 110–13. As is clear from her title, Lorde in this essay had serious reservations about the effectiveness of working inside the system.
9. Renita J. Weems, *Just a Sister Away: A Womanist Vision of Women's Relationships in the Bible* (San Diego: LuraMedia, 1988), 99.
10. Carol Lakey Hess, *Caretakers of Our Common House: Women's Development in Communities of Faith* (Nashville: Abingdon Press, 1997), 25.
11. Ibid., 28.
12. Ibid.

# Chapter Four

# Michal, Abigail, and Bathsheba: In the Eye of the Beholder

## 2 Samuel 11–12; 1 Kings 1–2 (Bathsheba) 1 Samuel 18:20–29; 19:8–17; 25:44; 2 Samuel 3:12–16; 6:16–23 (Michal) 1 Samuel 25:2–42 (Abigail)

I n this chapter we move back chronologically in Israel's history to the time of the beginning of monarchy. Michal, Abigail, and Bathsheba were three of King David's wives. He had other wives (five of the others are named with their offspring in 2 Sam. 3:2–5) and also, we are told, ten concubines (2 Sam. 15:16). But Michal, Abigail, and Bathsheba are the three about whom we have narrative information. According to the narrative, David first married Michal, then Abigail, and finally Bathsheba. There were no divorces; in accordance with Israelite custom for royalty, he had numerous wives at the same time. Yet their stories give us no clue about whether they ever met one another or interacted with each other. Thus we consider each of their stories individually.

In the discussion of wives in the previous chapters, I have alluded frequently to matters the storyteller does not spell out, points in the stories where we cannot be sure about cultural assumptions, the motivation of the characters, or other details. Understanding David's wives requires close attention to similar sorts of gaps in the information the text gives us. We will see how different ideas used by readers to fill in these gaps in information make a huge difference in our perception of these women. Is Bathsheba a seductress or a victim? Is Michal a pawn in a political system, a woman driven by emotions, or both? Is Abigail a scheming opportunist or a wise woman?[1]

Although Bathsheba is the last of the three to appear in David's life, we begin with her, since her story is more familiar to most people, and the value of paying special attention to the gaps in the story may therefore be easier to appreciate.

## Bathsheba

### *The Biblical Narrative*

The biblical narrative about Bathsheba appears in two places in the Old Testament, in 2 Samuel 11–12 and 1 Kings 1–2. The story begins when David sees Bathsheba, inquires after her identity, summons her, and she comes to him. When she later reports to him that she is pregnant, David arranges for her husband, Uriah, to return home from war in the hopes that he will sleep with her. But David's plan fails, so he arranges for Uriah's death. He then marries Bathsheba and their son is born. The prophet Nathan tells David that God is displeased with him and that his child will die. Despite David's pleas, the child does die, but another child is born to David and Bathsheba, Solomon, who will become David's successor.

We hear nothing about Bathsheba again until David is on his deathbed and a dispute arises over who will succeed to the throne. One faction supports Solomon, the other supports Adonijah, an older son of David by his wife Haggith. When Adonijah makes a move to seize power, Nathan enlists Bathsheba to approach David on behalf of her son Solomon, and David orders that Solomon be chosen over Adonijah. After David's death, Adonijah asks Bathsheba to intercede with Solomon on what seems to be a personal matter. When she presents the request to Solomon, however, he declares that Adonijah's proposal is really a subversive scheme and has him put to death.

## *Bathsheba: A Love Bride?*

What happens in the biblical account about Bathsheba, at least in the first part in 2 Samuel 11–12, may seem well known. But its very familiarity creates a problem and a challenge. Popular accounts in movies, historic artwork, and even children's Bible stories (if children's books dare tell this story at all) have filled in the gaps in information to such an extent that it is difficult for us to let go of our preconceptions and recognize what the text actually tells us and what it does not say. Therefore, we must read attentively to overcome our own assumptions about the relationship between David and Bathsheba.

The story opens, "[It was] in the spring of the year, the time when kings go out to battle." In the ancient Near East, military expeditions were normally undertaken in springtime. It is also possible, though the text focuses elsewhere, that springtime, as in our own culture, was traditionally associated with the rise of sexual passion (see Song of Sol. 2:10–13). The purpose of the battle reference in the introduction, of course, is to prepare us for the fact that Bathsheba's husband Uriah, a military officer, is away from Jerusalem with the army. The oddity is that King David has remained in Jerusalem. Biblical and ancient Near Eastern battle stories suggest that kings normally went out to fight with their troops, and we are not told why David has remained behind. But thus the stage is set.

David, walking about on his roof, sees a woman bathing; the narrator reports that she was very beautiful. So

> David sent someone to inquire about the woman. It was reported, "This is Bathsheba daughter of Eliam, the wife of Uriah the Hittite." So David sent messengers to get her, and she came to him, and he lay with her. (Now she was purifying herself after her period.) Then she returned to her house. The woman conceived; and she sent and told David, "I am pregnant." (2 Sam. 11:3–5)

Immediately we are faced with two important gaps in the narrative and thus in our information. First, how is it that David was able to see Bathsheba while she was bathing? Second, how exactly did Bathsheba "come" to David?

Concerning the first gap, many people assume that it is surely Bathsheba's fault that David sees her. Since it was presumably normal for people to go out on their rooftops, they assume that Bathsheba was not careful and behaved immodestly by bathing where she could be seen. Some have even suggested that Bathsheba deliberately bathed where she was sure King David would observe her, in hopes of attracting his sexual attentions. But the text does not comment on this point, and various other explanations are equally plausible. Perhaps David was peering around or through branches or vines, and the line of sight to Bathsheba was not easy or direct except by such efforts. Perhaps it was assumed by etiquette of the time that those on their rooftops looked out but not down, so as to preserve the privacy of others. Notice that contrary to the way the story is depicted in movies and paintings, Bathsheba is not reported to be bathing on another roof, and the direction David looks is not specified.

Another possibility occurred to me during my travels in a crowded area of Manila. Walking through a garden area early one morning I encountered a man bathing. He was in a partially secluded area, but it was the only place he had; clearly it was my responsibility in that context to keep moving, not stare, in effect pretend to see nothing. So also Bathsheba may have been in the most private place available to her for bathing. The important points are that (1) the text gives no indication that she was deliberately letting herself be seen, and (2) no matter how David happened to see her, it was his choice to avert his eyes or to take other action.

David finds out who she is and realizes that her husband is away at war. "So David sent messengers to get her, and she came to him, and he lay with her." Again, the text is much briefer than our imaginations, and we must give attention to this second gap in information. The text says only that the messengers "get" Bathsheba and she "comes" to David. Popular tradition presents us with a romantic love scene. We are led by the narrator to view the event from David's perspective. It reads like a male fantasy: the beautiful woman seen across a crowded room is immediately available for a night of passion—except that the fantasy is real this time. Women tend to buy into this fantasy as well—in our culture and many others women are socialized to dream of being noticed at an unexpected time and place as the pathway to ultimate relational happiness; marital status often stays conveniently in the background of such a fantasy.

But the gaps in the biblical text allow for a much different story. Did Bathsheba come willingly? The fantasy of instant romance with a stranger requires that the answer be yes, and it is fueled by the erotic interpretations of the opening bathing scene. But the equal likelihood is that Bathsheba may have wanted to say "No" but dared not. She was the wife of a foreign mercenary in the king's army; whether she herself was an Israelite or a foreigner by birth is not certain, but the foreign status of her Hittite husband is clear. The power differential between the king and any ordinary woman, including the wife of a foreign military officer, especially if she herself were not Israelite, would have been huge.

The absence of any report that Bathsheba protested does not prove she was not dismayed and frightened by the king's request. What might happen to one who disobeyed the king's summons? Was she even told what David had in mind? Possibly she was certain of his intentions only after her arrival in his house. Since the narrator is focused only on David's desire for her, we learn nothing of Bathsheba's view of her situation. The narrator reports only that "he lay with her . . . Then she returned to her house" (2 Sam. 11:4).

Everything might have remained undiscovered, except—"the woman conceived." And she sent word to David. Since she had been "purifying herself after her period" (v. 4) and her husband was away at war, the pregnancy must be by David. In the next sections of the story, Bathsheba disappears as David first tries to get her husband to have sex with her, then when that plan fails arranges for her husband's murder. The narrator, whose focus is David, returns to Bathsheba only to report in a few words that she lamented her dead husband (v. 26). Then when the period of mourning was over, "David sent and brought her to his house, and she became his wife, and bore him a son" (v. 27). We are not told how long the period of mourning was; we do not know about that in Israelite custom. Obviously it was less than nine months, since the child conceived before Uriah died was born after David took Bathsheba as his wife.

There are other gaps in the text, as well. Some interpreters have suggested that Bathsheba is glad to be rid of her husband, and her lamenting of his death is mere crocodile tears. It is also supposed that she was eager to continue the alleged romance by marrying David.[2] But neither of these points is made in the text. There is no reason to suppose that her lament over her husband is not genuine. And the circumstances of her pregnancy may have left her no other option than to marry David, given her cultural context. In fact, it seems doubtful that she would have been given any choice in the matter. Note also that contrary to popular depictions of the story, the text records no sexual contact between David and Bathsheba prior to their marriage other than the initial encounter in which she became pregnant.

The story, as it continues in 2 Samuel 12, tends to exonerate Bathsheba, placing the blame squarely on David, as in 12:1 we read, "But the thing that David had done displeased the LORD, and the LORD sent Nathan to David." The prophet Nathan, one of David's key supporters and advisers, tells David a story about a rich man with a huge flock of sheep who steals his poor neighbor's only lamb to prepare as a feast for visitors. As David announces the guilt of the rich man, Nathan responds, "You are the man!" (12:7). Bathsheba is not implicated by the narrator, who says God is displeased with what "David" had done. And Nathan's parable likewise focuses on David, who in his lust and greed has stolen what belonged to Uriah. To hear the voice and understand what is going on in the heart of Bathsheba, whose name is mentioned only by the messengers who report to King David, to hear Bathsheba who in this chapter says not a word except, via a messenger, "I am pregnant," I believe we must recognize that she may likely have been a trapped woman rather than a willing participant or the initiator of a clandestine relationship.

My mother, at age eighty-seven, remembered only one thing about this story: her baby died. Yes, in fulfillment of Nathan's prophecy "The LORD struck the child that Uriah's wife bore to David, and it became very ill. . . . On the seventh day the child died" (2 Sam. 12:15, 18). Again the story focuses on David, and the phrase "that Uriah's wife bore" reinforces David's wrongdoing. We are told in detail of David's pleading for the child; but the narrator is uninterested in Bathsheba and she disappears totally from the narrative until after the child dies. We hear nothing at all of her actions or feelings during the baby's illness. After the child dies, David, still the narrator's focus, consoles Bathsheba and lies with her, and she bears a second son, Solomon.

Many Christians today would disagree with the idea that God punishes adults by killing their children, or that God's judgment cannot be changed by confession and penitence (12:13–17). But the issue I raise here with regard to Bathsheba is not what God did or did not do, but rather what the narrator of the story does not do. The narrator, focused on David, does not consider what the baby's mother may or may not have felt. What difference would it have made to her whether the child was conceived in love or in fear? That it was conceived while Uriah was alive? That she is now married to David, whether in love or in fear?

As we ask about Bathsheba, we realize more and more how little we know of her. In our own time, we may honor her by recognizing how little we know, by keeping in mind the great power differential between her and David, and by realizing that the negative portrayals of her that are familiar to us are not necessarily supported by the biblical text.

### Bathsheba: Queen Mother

Bathsheba is not mentioned again until the time of David's death, when she appears in a position of relative power within David's court, as the mother of the favored (although not the eldest) son, Solomon. In contrast to the story in 2 Samuel, here she has a significant active and speaking role. Even so, her action here in 1 Kings 1 is still not of her own initiative, but is in response to the advice of the prophet Nathan, who tells her what to do to "save [her] own life and the life of [her] son Solomon" (1 Kgs. 1:12).

David is old and ill. Two factions are struggling in a potentially deadly feud to succeed him. Adonijah has already made a move to become David's successor, but Nathan favors Solomon and develops a counterstrategy in Solomon's support. He convinces Bathsheba to complain to David about Adonijah's action, thereby paving the way for his own complaint against Adonijah. Bathsheba's role consists of telling David about Adonijah's actions and asking David to announce specifically which son (by implication, Solomon) he designates as successor. After Nathan seconds her report, David announces to Bathsheba that her son Solomon shall be his rightful successor, and he makes the necessary arrangements for such a proclamation.

After David's death and as the mother of the new king, Bathsheba seems to have a special place in palace affairs, a place similar to that of several other queen mothers known from biblical tradition and ancient Near Eastern sources.[3] Adonijah, the loser in the power struggle, approaches her rather than anyone else in the court and asks her to intercede with Solomon on his behalf regarding a personal matter: he wants to marry the concubine Abishag, who had been David's companion in his old age. We sense that the tension between the factions continues, as Bathsheba initiates their conversation with a question: "Do you come peaceably?" and Adonijah replies that he lost the kingship to his brother because "it was his from the LORD" (1 Kgs. 2:13–15). Satisfied, Bathsheba agrees to "speak to the king on [Adonijah's] behalf" (2:18).

She goes to Solomon. Clearly Solomon respects her, for he bows to her and has a separate throne brought for her to sit upon (v. 19). She says, "I have one small request to make of you; do not refuse me" (2:20), and Solomon says he will not refuse. She continues, "Let Abishag the Shunammite be given to your brother Adonijah as his wife" (v. 21). Marriage to the previous king's concubine meant that one acquired royal authority, and Solomon interprets this marriage request as Adonijah's strategy for usurping the throne. He replies, "And why do you ask Abishag the Shunammite for Adonijah? Ask for him the kingdom as well!" (v. 22).

At this point, Solomon decrees death for his rival, and Bathsheba abruptly and permanently disappears from the narrative.

How should we assess Bathsheba's role here? What she says to Solomon in their meeting is far from transparent, and interpreting it depends upon how we imagine her tone of voice, to which of course we have no access. Some surmise she was duped by Adonijah and really did not understand affairs of state enough to realize that in her culture marriage to a king's concubine meant the assertion of royal authority and thus that Adonijah's true goal was to usurp Solomon's power. This possibility seems the least likely to me. Others suppose that she recognized Adonijah's ulterior motive and relayed his request to Solomon in anticipation that Solomon also would see through the ruse; perhaps she used her tone of voice to indicate that she did not really expect Solomon to grant her request. Still others imagine that her manner of speaking hinted to Solomon that he should dispose of Adonijah.

Whatever we make of Bathsheba in this second part of her story, we notice three things about how she is portrayed: First, she is no longer silent. She speaks in the royal presence first of her husband David, then of her son Solomon, and she is treated deferentially. Second, despite her new outspokenness, the narrator is still interested in the king and succession to the throne; he does not give us access to Bathsheba's thoughts as she decided whether and how to comply with requests made of her, and Bathsheba disappears each time as soon as her part is finished. Finally, she is still portrayed as a relatively dependent and less powerful person than the men around her. In each instance she acts in accord with what a man has asked her to do and say. She appears only when responding to the concerns and wishes of others. In sum, Bathsheba the queen mother has power, but she does not function as an independent agent; the narrator's male focus obscures her true self from our view.

## Michal

The issues of power differential and the narrator's perspective continue as we turn to the story of Michal, David's first wife. Michal figures in stories about David reported in 1 Samuel 18:20–29;

19:8–17; 25:44; 2 Samuel 3:12–16; 6:16–23. In studying Michal's story, it is important to keep in mind that it belongs to a partisan account of the history of David's rise to power and kingship, a history that involves many conflicts with his predecessor, King Saul. The narrator, possibly a member of the court of David or Solomon, has a pro-David, anti-Saul viewpoint throughout.

### The Biblical Narrative

Michal is a daughter of King Saul. The young hero David with God's help wins victories against Philistines and other enemies and gains renown among the populace, thus threatening Saul's leadership. Saul of course hopes to have one of his own sons succeed to the throne, rather than have his line displaced by the upstart David. So he sets a trap, proposing to David an alliance through David's marriage to his daughter Michal but requiring that the marriage present be "a hundred foreskins of the Philistines" (1 Sam. 18:25). Saul expects David will be killed in battle with the Philistines, but David prevails and the marriage takes place. Saul tries again, however, sending his own men to murder David. With Michal's help, David escapes and continues to elude Saul, who later gives Michal to another husband named Palti.

When David becomes king after Saul's death, he demands that Michal be returned to him (2 Sam. 3:14) as part of a political deal with Saul's military leader Abner. Eventually King David captures Jerusalem, a city Israel had not held until then, and he plans to make it his capital. This plan includes a religious procession in which the ark of the covenant (the box made in the wilderness under Moses' direction that contained the tablets of the Ten Commandments) is brought to Jerusalem, called in the story the "city of David." As the procession arrives in the city, Michal sees David dancing before the ark and "despise[s]" him (2 Sam. 6:16). When David returns home after the celebration, she castigates him for "uncovering" himself "before the eyes of his servants' maids" (v. 20). David replies in vehement defense of himself, and the narrator concludes the story of Michal with the statement that "the daughter of Saul had no child to the day of her death" (v. 23).

## Michal: A Political Pawn?

If the narrator thinks of Bathsheba as David's love bride late in his career, the narrator's interest in Michal is as the early bride destined to make or break political alliances. The use of women in marriages to consolidate political alliances and power is known in every era of recorded history, and in tribal cultures as well as in nation-states. We know it from a variety of other examples in the Bible, notably Solomon's marriage to an Egyptian princess (1 Kgs. 3:1) and Ahab's marriage to Jezebel, daughter of the King of Sidon (1 Kgs. 16:31). In the case of Michal, however, the custom takes a peculiar twist, as we will see.

The stage is set in 1 Samuel 18:20–25: Saul's intent in arranging the marriage is not really to consolidate an alliance with David but rather to engineer the death of David, whom Saul perceives as a dangerous rival. Michal for her part is reported to "love" David. The narrator indicates in verses 20–21 that Michal's love somehow suits Saul's purposes, although it is not clear how her feelings make any difference to his initial plan against David. The narrator never indicates that Michal knows about Saul's deal with David concerning the marriage, or that David loves or has any feeling for Michal. As Cheryl Exum points out, the reference to Michal's love for David is noteworthy, for nowhere else in the entire Hebrew Bible does a narrator explicitly report that a woman "loves" a man.[4] No woman who is being used for political purpose can be neutral, and we wonder whether Michal will support her father, as tradition requires, or her husband, as "love" would suggest. In any case, we can expect heightened drama.

The narrator explains that Saul's request for one hundred foreskins from dead Philistines as the wedding present is intended to bring about David's death (18:25). And we assume from this that Saul has no more regard for the feelings of his daughter who loves David than he has for the life of his rival. Of course the plan does not work. The hero David meets Saul's demand, and Saul is forced to go through with his side of the bargain.

Once the marriage takes place, Saul has even more trouble than before. His dual fears that both God and Michal are with David are quickly realized. First, David again defeats the Philistines (18:30), proving that God is allied with him, and then Michal contrives to save David from Saul's next murderous plan. Although Saul has promised his son Jonathan that he will not harm David (19:1–7), he sends assassins to David's home, instructing them to attack in the morning (19:11). Michal discovers the danger and helps David escape through a window. To delay discovery that he is gone, she prepares a dummy in his bed and claims that he is ill. When Saul confronts her about what he regards as treachery against him, Michal defends her actions by claiming that David had threatened her life.

Then, without explanation, some years later this woman who was said to love her husband and who in a crisis chose her husband over her father turns harshly against her husband (2 Sam. 6:16–23). What has happened? The narrator, focused as always on David's adventures in his rise to kingship, does not give us much help with this question. Although we cannot be sure, the answer may lie somewhere in Michal's experiences during those intervening years. At some point in those years "Saul had given his daughter Michal, David's wife, to Palti son of Laish, who was from Gallim" (1 Sam. 25:44). We are told nothing of Saul's motive; we know nothing of Michal's reaction, or when David learned about this marriage, or who Palti may have been.

Scholars speculate that Saul was acting in response to Michal's support of David and that he wanted to weaken David's rising political power by undoing the political alliance built by his marriage to Michal.[5] If this speculation is correct, Michal is once more the pawn in political machinations. This interpretation is supported by David's subsequent demand that "Saul's daughter Michal . . . my wife" be returned to him as part of a political deal in which Saul's followers finally throw their support to David (2 Sam. 3:12–16). David refers to her both as "Saul's daughter" and as "my wife," and he recalls specifically the price of one hundred Philistine foreskins, thus emphasizing that she belongs to him and that he is in control over a surviving member of Saul's family. While the narrator notes that Palti followed along crying behind Michal, we are given no indication of Michal's feelings.

David wants her, so she is brought to him. At this point we do not
know whether she "loves" him or has other feelings. She is once
again simply a part of a political agreement.[6]

And so we come to the scene of David dancing before the ark
of the covenant. Michal sees him from the window and "despise[s]
him in her heart" (2 Sam. 6:16). Her love has apparently turned
to hate. After the ceremonies are completed, she meets David with
words of sarcasm:

> "How the king of Israel honored himself today, uncovering
> himself today before the eyes of his servants' maids, as any
> vulgar fellow might shamelessly uncover himself!" (6:20).

David replies,

> "It was before the LORD, who chose me in place of your
> father . . . that I have danced before the LORD. . . . By the
> maids of whom you have spoken, by them I shall be held in
> honor" (vv. 21–22).

A close look at this exchange suggests, as Exum observes,[7] that
much more is at stake than whether David was dancing scantily
clothed. Michal refers to him disparagingly as "king of Israel" and
David's reply focuses on how God chose him as king, clearly alluding to that choice being at the expense of Saul, Michal's father.
Perhaps by now she has finally realized the extent to which she has
been a pawn of both Saul and David. Thus it is scarcely acciden-
tal that the narrator refers to her repeatedly as "daughter of Saul"
in this paragraph, but not as "wife of David," which was used when
she aided David's escape from her father. Each time Michal is portrayed as taking action on her own, her life and identity are con-
strained by the ongoing dispute over Israel's leadership.

Finally, the narrator informs us that Michal "daughter of Saul"
had no child to the day of her death (6:23). Thus ends her story.
Is this final note simply an added fact, separate from the sharp
words that have just been spoken? Why is Michal childless? Is
her childlessness to be understood as an outcome of the bitter

exchange of taunts? Did God strike her with barrenness because she spoke against the Lord's anointed? Did David refuse any further sexual relations with her because of this angry exchange? Is it possible that Michal herself refused to have anything further to do with David?

Although some feminist readers have proposed that Michal refused David, I suspect one of the first two meanings was more likely on the narrator's mind. As the reporter of David's rise to power, the narrator is pro-David, anti-Saul; the narrator would not want to leave unanswered such an insult to King David as Saul's daughter has uttered.

Michal's barrenness has one additional and significant consequence: it ensures that David will father no offspring who could trace their ancestry to Saul's line. The discontinuity between Saul's line and David's is complete; no one of Saulide background can ever lay claim to succession to David's throne. Back in 1 Samuel 15, before David was ever even mentioned, the narrator told the story of Saul's failure to keep God's commands and God's rejection of Saul. The prophet Samuel told Saul, "Because you have rejected the word of the LORD, he has also rejected you from being king" (15:23). The utter finality of this divine decision is confirmed in the childlessness of Michal.

To the very end, Michal remains a character whose destiny is determined by others. Yet in her actions, as in Bathsheba's conferring with David, Adonijah, and Solomon, we see a woman who makes some effort to shape her future. She defies her father, rescues her husband, and eventually defies her husband. She is a woman of emotion, as is seen in her "love" for David and in her biting sarcasm to him as she exits the stage of the story. Yet we learn far less of her story than we might like. As I mourn with Bathsheba over the deaths of Uriah and her baby boy, I mourn with Palti over Michal's fate.

## Abigail

We turn finally to the story of Abigail, whose story is the least known of these three wives of David. Neither a wife of illicit passion like Bathsheba, nor of political expedience like Michal, Abigail typifies the wife of down-to-earth common sense. Her story is presented in 1 Samuel 25, and takes place in the time after Michal aided David's escape. He is living on the outskirts of society and building his power base.

### The Biblical Narrative

David sends messengers to Nabal, a man of wealth, requesting food and drink for himself and his supporters. Nabal rudely denies the request, and in response David sets out to attack Nabal and his family and servants. One of David's messengers informs Nabal's wife Abigail of the impending attack. Without informing Nabal, Abigail rides out to meet David and his men, bringing with her the food and drink David requested. She apologizes for Nabal at length, praises David, and asks to be remembered when he finally succeeds. David thanks her for her action, which has averted his bloodthirsty plan, and accepts her gifts. When Abigail returns home and tells Nabal what has happened, he is undone: "his heart died within him; he became like a stone" (25:37). Soon God strikes Nabal dead, and David rejoices that God has avenged the insult he suffered at Nabal's hand. He then sends messengers to Abigail to announce his intention to marry her, and she goes to David and becomes his wife.

### Abigail: Opportunist or Peacemaker?

The narrator's introduction to this remarkable story sets up two of the principal characters:

> Now the name of the man was Nabal, and the name of his wife Abigail. The woman was clever and beautiful, but the man was surly and mean. (25:3)

At this point in the story of David, he is living as an outlaw in a southern wilderness region, building a following in the style of Robin Hood. The message David sends to Nabal (whose name means "fool") begins with "peace" but immediately points out that Nabal has suffered no trouble or economic losses from David's men. The message implies that it is time for Nabal to show his appreciation by handing over the requested supplies. What will happen next has been established by the characterization of Nabal as surly and mean and, sure enough, he sends back an insolent message:

> "Who is David? . . . Shall I take my bread and my water . . . and give it to men who come from I do not know where?" (25:10–11).

These words are not only surly, but foolhardy (as we expect from Nabal's name), and David sets out immediately to fight against Nabal.

Abigail to the rescue: with great supplies of meat, grain, and fruit she sets out to intercept David. David has become angrier and angrier, pledging to wipe out Nabal's people to the last man (vv. 21–22), when suddenly Abigail presents herself before David, dismounting her donkey and bowing to the ground. She enters into an extended speech:

> My lord, do not take seriously this ill-natured fellow, Nabal; for as his name is, so is he; . . . but I, your servant, did not see the young men of my lord, whom you sent.
>
> Now then, my lord, as the LORD lives, and as you yourself live, since the LORD has restrained you from bloodguilt and from taking vengeance with your own hand, now let your enemies and those who seek to do evil to my lord be like Nabal. And now let this present that your servant has brought to my lord be given to the young men who follow my lord. Please forgive the trespass of your servant; for the LORD will certainly make my lord a sure house, because my lord is fighting the battles of the LORD; and evil shall not be found in you so long as you live. If anyone should rise up to pursue you and to seek your life, the life of my lord shall be bound in the bundle of the living under the care of the LORD

your God; but the lives of your enemies he shall sling out as from the hollow of a sling. When the LORD has done to my lord according to all the good that he has spoken concerning you, and has appointed you prince over Israel, my lord shall have no cause of grief, or pangs of conscience, for having shed blood without cause or for having saved himself. And when the LORD has dealt well with my lord, then remember your servant. (25:25–31)

In this speech, Abigail begins by asking David to ignore Nabal's response; then she continues as if David's plan for attack were already canceled, giving the LORD the credit for that turn of events. Perhaps we are to imagine that something in David's demeanor leads her to say this; but perhaps she is using a rhetorically effective strategy of speaking as if the hoped-for result were already in place. She then offers her gifts and suggests that God will protect David and take vengeance on any of David's enemies so that David can remain free of bloodguilt.

The center of her speech contains phrases that would be called prophecy if they came from the mouths of the official prophets of David's time, Nathan or Samuel. Most notable is her comment, "the LORD will certainly make my lord a sure house" (that is, a dynasty; v. 28), which anticipates the promise given to David through Nathan years later, after David has become king in Jerusalem. At that time, David decides to build a "house" (that is, a temple) for the Lord. Through the prophet Nathan, however, David learns that the Lord does not wish him to build such a "house" (temple). Instead, Nathan announces, using words nearly identical to Abigail's, that "the LORD will make [David] a house" (meaning a dynasty; 2 Sam. 7:11). Thus even while David was in hiding from Saul at the very beginning of his career, long before David became king, Abigail declared God's promise of a Davidic dynasty.

Abigail concludes with a remark or request that may be merely conventional speech, but may also be intended as a deliberate signal to David that her loyalty would be to him rather than to her husband: "When the LORD . . . has appointed you prince over Israel, . . . when the LORD has dealt well with my lord, then remember your servant" (25:30–31).

David in reply blesses God for sending Abigail, and blesses her "good sense" (25:33) that has kept him from bloodguilt. Abigail returns home, and the next morning, after Nabal recovers from a drunken stupor, she tells him what has transpired. When he dies ten days later, David is satisfied that God has avenged Nabal's insult, and thus Abigail's statement that "the LORD has restrained [David] from . . . taking vengeance" (25:26) is confirmed. Immediately David sends messengers to fetch Abigail for marriage. David has "remembered" her as she had asked that he do, much sooner than she suggested, for he is still a long time away from becoming "prince [ruler] of Israel." Although she speaks of herself as a slave to David's servants (25:41), she is herself obviously a woman of wealth, with five maids in attendance (v. 42) as she rides off to become David's wife.

Is Abigail the sensible woman who tried to protect not only her household but David as well, or is she an opportunist who sees and seizes her chance to attach herself to a rising power? Is David's marriage to Abigail advantageous primarily because it gives him the wealth and landholdings of the dead Nabal, or does it provide him a woman of wise counsel by his side? The text does not decide these questions for us, and in fact it allows for complex motivations, rather than forcing us to choose one to the exclusion of the other. We do note that sexuality does not play any role in the narrative of this relationship; Abigail is neither barren like Michal nor the focus of desire like Bathsheba. A summary note concerning six of David's wives and their offspring reports that Abigail had a son named Chileab (2 Sam. 3:3), but he plays no role in the subsequent narrative, and neither he nor Abigail is ever mentioned again. In effect her story ends with her marriage to David.

For all that Abigail takes strong action to protect the men of her husband's household from the consequences of his action, for all that she is pictured anticipating David's future role, and for all of her sensibility, decisiveness, and generosity (or perhaps her savvy in recognizing what is necessary in dealing with outlaws), some people find it more difficult to appreciate Abigail than to sympathize with Bathsheba or Michal. As Alice Bach says, Abigail "refers to her husband as a fool, sides with his enemy, and does not even mourn his death."[8] By that measure she is far from being a loyal and devoted wife. But perhaps this assessment does not take seriously what a fool Nabal really was, based on his actions and on the narrator's matter-of-fact statement that Nabal was surly and mean, even as Abigail was clever and beautiful. If today we challenge the assumption that a wife should automatically side with a surly and mean husband, we should not demand more from Abigail. And her rescue of many servants of her household from certain death at David's hands deserves celebration.

Judette Gallares, a Filipina Roman Catholic nun, draws our attention to larger ethical dimensions of Abigail's intervention to prevent violence against her household. Gallares presents Abigail as "a faithful pacifist, an advocate of active non-violence and peace, [who] offers us an alternative value system, another set of ideals, another approach to leadership that relies more on the power of peace and reconciliation than on the power of hate and vengeance."[9] Gallares finds in Abigail's speech to David an "intuitive" application of four principles of active nonviolence used in the economic and political resistance movements in her native Philippines:

1. Recognizing any truth or goodness in the adversary's position
2. Admitting any ways in which one has betrayed that goodness of the adversary
3. Pointing out how everyone (including the adversary) will be badly affected by the adversary's proposed course of action
4. Proposing how the adversary can participate in developing an alternative solution to the conflict[10]

If we assess Abigail's speech in such terms, then the image of Abigail as the clever but possibly callous opportunist wife fades and the image of a courageous peacemaking woman gains ascendancy. Gallares concludes by relating Abigail's action and words in 1 Samuel 25 to Paul's exhortation in Romans 12:

> Hate what is evil, hold fast to what is good. . . . Bless those who persecute you; bless and do not curse them. Rejoice with those who rejoice, weep with those who weep. Live in harmony with one another; do not be haughty, but associate with the lowly; do not claim to be wiser than you are. Do not repay anyone evil for evil, but take thought for what is noble in the sight of all. If it is possible, so far as it depends on you, live peaceably with all. Beloved, never avenge yourselves, but leave room for the wrath of God; for it is written, "Vengeance is mine, I will repay, says the Lord." No, "if your enemies are hungry, feed them; if they are thirsty, give them something to drink; for by doing this you will heap burning coals on their heads." Do not be overcome by evil, but overcome evil with good. (Rom. 12:9, 14–21)

For me, this juxtaposing of Paul's words with Abigail's speech gives her words a new theological depth. She does not approach David just to hitch herself to a rising star or even just to save her own household; rather, she seeks to bring an end to a cycle of rendering evil for evil, so that peace may prevail over vengeance. I realize that for me Gallares's view of Abigail is persuasive partly because of my own experience in the Philippines, getting to know women and men who like Abigail actually had gone out to meet the advancing hostile forces, who placed their bodies and their words of persuasion and prayer between foolish and angry forces, and contrary to all my cynical human logic, saw transformation take place. Of course, active nonviolence does not always work. I scarcely met a person in the Philippines who had not lost a personal friend or relative to the internal strife in that country. Yet their stories of the times active nonviolence did work kindled anew my belief in miracles—experiences of abiding astonishment at the power of God at work for justice and peace.

### Concluding Reflection

At the beginning of this chapter I pointed out that each of these three wives of David appears in the Bible in narrative isolation, with no indication that they had any contact or even knowledge of one another, and I have presented them to you separately, to match that aspect of the text. In each case I have described competing interpretations of their stories: Bathsheba as active seducer, as cooperative lover, or as trapped and powerless victim, as a queen mother of power or one manipulated by others; Michal as one who loves and who hates, as one active toward her own interests, or as one used as a political pawn; Abigail as an opportunist, as a defender of her family's interests, or as a prophetic voice and God-fearing advocate of nonviolence.

These women, like those we have considered in previous chapters, need to be allowed to have their narrative complexity. We should not try to reduce them or confine them to just one of the interpretive options. In the same way, as we think of women today, we should resist reductionist stereotyping or pigeonholing of ourselves, our friends, or any women, striving instead to recognize and honor the complexity of our human interactions.

## Questions for Individual Reflection or Group Study

1. Chapter 3 on Esther and Vashti included an imaginary conversation between the two women, using the Jewish tradition of creative imagination, or midrash. In that same tradition, imagine that Bathsheba, Michal, and Abigail are sitting together in the women's courtyard of the Jerusalem palace and begin to reminisce. What do you imagine they might say to each other?
2. Which of the three wives of David do you think raises the most pertinent concerns for women today? Why?
3. In what ways has your picture of David changed as a result of learning more about these three wives?
4. How do you think differences in power affect marriage relationships today? Compare your thoughts about today with your understanding of how lack of power affected the lives of David's wives.
5. Do you think that women have a greater tendency to be peacemakers than men, or is this a cultural stereotype?

What do you mean by "peacemaker" as you answer this question?

6. How do we tend to "flatten out" or stereotype or ignore the complexity of people when we tell stories about them? Why do we do that? Does the biblical narrator's tendency to do this make you feel that such a practice is acceptable, or inevitable, or to be resisted? Does the answer vary depending on why the story is being told?

## Notes

1. In this chapter I am drawing especially upon the work of J. Cheryl Exum, *Fragmented Women: Feminist (Sub)Versions of Biblical Narratives* (Valley Forge, Pa.: Trinity Press International, 1993) and Alice Bach, "The Pleasure of Her Text," in *The Pleasure of Her Text: Feminist Readings of Biblical and Historical Texts* (ed. Alice Bach; Philadelphia: Trinity Press International, 1990), 25–44.
2. These are features of the plotline of the 1985 Paramount Pictures film *King David*. See discussion in J. Cheryl Exum, *Plotted, Shot, and Painted: Cultural Representations of Biblical Women* (Sheffield: Sheffield Academic Press, 1996), 23–24.
3. See Elna Solvang, *A Woman's Place Is in the House: Royal Women of Judah and Their Involvement in the House of David* (JSOTSup 349; London: Sheffield Academic Press, 2003).
4. Exum, *Fragmented Women*, 43.
5. Ibid., 23.
6. Ibid., 45–46.
7. Exum, *Plotted, Shot, and Painted*, 61.
8. Bach, "The Pleasure of Her Text," 34.
9. Judette A. Gallares, *Images of Faith: Spirituality of Women in the Old Testament* (Maryknoll, N.Y.: Orbis Books, 1992), 124.
10. Ibid., 125.

# Chapter Five

# Gomer: Who Betrayed Whom?

## Hosea 1–3

Gomer was the wife of the prophet Hosea, who delivered his message to Israel in about 730 B.C.E. Hosea's message focused on Israel's failure to remain faithful to Yahweh alone, for the people were worshiping other gods and the political leadership was engaged in murderous intrigue and foreign alliances. Hosea announced that God would bring terrible judgment of political disaster upon the people, but also promised that there was hope for Israel's future with God after the time of punishment.

In Hosea's time, Israel understood its relationship to God through the metaphor of a great king and his subjects, and used the word "covenant" for this relationship. When Israel worshiped other gods or joined in alliance with nations that worshiped other gods, they showed disloyalty to God as their King and thus violated the covenant. Hosea did not reject this imagery, but he wanted to emphasize the more personal and intimate aspects of God's covenant with Israel. To do this, he developed additional metaphors from family life, portraying God and Israel as parent and child (chap. 11) and as husband and wife (chaps. 1–3). In each case, God (the parent or husband) is pictured as faithful, while Israel is portrayed as wayward, disobedient, or unfaithful.

In developing the metaphor of God as husband and Israel as wife, Hosea introduced the story of his marriage with Gomer. Her name actually appears only once in the text (1:3), and Hosea was much more interested in developing his metaphor about God and Israel as husband and wife than he was in giving us any details about Gomer. The one thing we can say for sure is that she is portrayed as a woman who engages in sex outside of marriage. As we will see, this absence of detail has led to many different theories about Gomer's background and behavior. Some interpreters have even wondered whether she was a real person.

It is not possible to assess the theories about Gomer without giving close attention to Hosea's own main interest, the metaphor of God as divine husband. What did it mean for Hosea to think of God as Israel's husband? How does he portray God in the role of husband? How does God as husband behave when his people are unfaithful in this metaphorical marriage relationship? Hosea is able to use the imagery to express some important theological insights, especially concerning how deeply God is hurt by the people's unfaithfulness. But today we may also see potential danger in Hosea's imagery, because a major aspect of it involves the husband's punishment of his wayward wife.

To gain a better perspective on these insights and dangers, we will need to explore ancient Israel's cultural conceptions of marriage, illicit sex, and prostitution, and how those conceptions still influence our views today. We will need to consider our own ideas of good and bad wives and good and bad husbands, and to think about how the biblical metaphor compares to those ideas. These are complicated issues, but they are critical to assessing the possible impact of Hosea's message on marriage and family life today.

After a review of the basic biblical material, we will turn to questions about Gomer's life and behavior; the contributions of Hosea's marriage imagery to our understanding of God; and the dangers inherent in that marriage imagery.

## The Biblical Material

Hosea 1 is written in the form of a third-person biographical statement about Hosea. The writer, whether Hosea or someone else who added the chapter as a preface, reports that God commanded Hosea to take a "wife of whoredom and have children of whore-

dom, for the land commits great whoredom by forsaking the
LORD" (1:2). In response to God's command Hosea married a
woman named Gomer; she bore three children, Jezreel ("God
sows"), Lo-ruhamah ("Not pitied") and Lo-ammi ("Not my people"). Each child was named by Hosea at God's command, and
each name symbolizes an aspect of the estranged relationship
between God and Israel. Although the story does not mention it,
we can imagine that whenever people heard Hosea's children
called by these names they would think of God's message proclaimed by the prophet.

Chapter 2 is a complex poetic interpretation of Hosea's marriage experience in relation to God's experience with Israel. God
speaks metaphorically as if in the role of a husband speaking to his
children, and to other people about his wife and children. God
begins by saying he will deal harshly with his wife if her whoring
does not stop (vv. 2–4); he describes the mother's behavior and
quotes what she has said about going to lovers (v. 5), then describes
consequences he will impose in order to bring her back to him
(vv. 6–7). He refers to her lack of appreciation for his gifts (v. 8)
and again identifies the punishment that will come upon her
because of her unfaithfulness, alluding specifically to worship of
other gods (vv. 9–13).

Verse 14 opens a new section. God, still portrayed as the husband, now describes how he will woo Israel back to him (vv.
14–15) and will establish a new covenant with a renewed marriage
relationship in which the wife will remain faithful (vv. 16–20). The
picture of this future relationship climaxes with a reversal of the
children's negative names to positive ones. God will have pity on
"Not pitied"; "Not my people" will be called "You are my people," and to this renaming the child will respond, "You are my
God" (vv. 21–23).

Chapter 3 is Hosea's first-person autobiographical account of
the story. He reports God's instruction to him to "love a woman
who has a lover and is an adulteress, just as the LORD loves the
people of Israel, though they turn to other gods" (3:1). He buys
her (she is not named), and keeps her without sexual relations
for a long period of time (3:2–3). This period without intimacy

appears to symbolize a period of exile for Israel, before the people finally return to God and experience God's goodness (vv. 4–5).

## What Can We Know about Gomer?

Most people who have heard of Gomer have probably assumed that the story took place more or less as described in the summary of chapters 1 and 3 above. That is my view as well. But it is important to realize that the story is not so straightforward as it first appears, and the complexities of the text have led to other theories. As we review some of these alternative views, we will see that readers' own discomfort with this story may affect their interpretations.

### *1. Was Gomer a Real Person?*

Scholars have debated for decades whether Gomer and her children were real historical people, or whether the story of Hosea's marriage was only an allegory. We cannot finally know the answer to this question, since there is no independent evidence outside these three chapters to help settle the debate.

I assume that Gomer was a real person to whom Hosea really was married, and that she did bear the three children named in the text. Those who disagree, believing that the story is an allegory, argue that God would not be so unreasonable as to require a good man (the prophet) to marry an immoral woman (Gomer), just to make a point to Israel. God did, however, require other prophets to do culturally unacceptable things, such as walk naked in the street (Isaiah), or never marry or attend funerals (Jeremiah), and commentators have not objected to these comparable demands. Perhaps viewing Hosea's marriage as allegorical rather than real helps interpreters to deal with their own aversion to the idea of such a marriage.

Assuming that Gomer was a real person, I also view the autobiography in chapter 3 as a continuation of the biographical report in chapter 1, and I assume that the woman referred to in chapter 3 is Gomer, even though her name is not mentioned. Here we see the prophet starting over again with his wife, despite her continuing promiscuity and separation from him. Some scholars view chapter 3 as a different description of the initial marriage described in chapter 1; but the period when the husband withholds sexual relations (3:3) does not fit well with that idea. Overall I think it is more likely that Hosea shocks his community a second time by restoring his relationship with the woman they thought he should never have married in the first place.

### 2. When Did Gomer Become Promiscuous?

Was Gomer already a promiscuous woman before her marriage, or did she instead have only a "tendency to promiscuity"?

Some scholars who accept the idea that Gomer was a historical person and not allegorical still argue that Gomer was a virgin when Hosea married her. They believe that the word "whoredom" in God's command (1:2) refers to a tendency rather than to actual behavior, and that Gomer became promiscuous only after the marriage. But the text does not say that God specifically chose Gomer for Hosea, and it is not clear how anyone—Hosea in his day or a person today—would be able to identify a virgin with such an alleged "tendency" toward illicit sex. It is part of our cultural lore that there are such women and that their future behavior can be anticipated, but this is lore rather than tested reality, and we do not know whether Israel had such a conception.

In contrast to this theory, the simplest meaning of Hosea 1:2 seems to be that God commanded Hosea to marry a woman who was already promiscuous. This traditional interpretation also fits with what we know from the lives of other prophets. Hosea's marrying a promiscuous woman is an example of an "acted sign," that is, a symbolic action or activity that directs the people's attention to some aspect of God's message. Prophets usually performed such "acted signs" in response to a direct command by God. The unusual actions of other prophets, which I mentioned earlier, are also examples of acted signs commanded by God: Jeremiah avoids funerals as an acted sign that there will be no time for funerals in the time of devastation God has called him to announce (Jer. 16:5–9); Isaiah goes naked through the streets as an acted sign that captives will be led away naked (Isaiah 20). As the Israelites see these actions taking place over time, God's message is regularly reinforced. In the same way, as Hosea and Gomer lived in their community, the character of their marriage relationship would serve as an acted sign, reinforcing over and over again Hosea's verbal message that Israel had acted unfaithfully in its covenant relationship to God.

### 3. Was Gomer a Prostitute?

What was the nature of Gomer's sexual activity outside of marriage? Three main theories have been proposed: (1) that she was a "sacred prostitute" who offered sex as part of a religious ritual; (2) that she was a common prostitute; and (3) that she engaged in illicit sex, but not for pay.

The first of these three options—that Gomer was a sacred prostitute—can almost surely be dismissed as incorrect. For nearly all of the twentieth century, scholars supposed that ancient Canaanite and Mesopotamian religions in Israel's time included "sacred prostitutes" among their female temple personnel. It was believed that men had sex with these women, perhaps as a fertility ritual, as a regular part of the worship practices at the sanctuaries dedicated to the gods of these religions. It was also assumed that true Israelite religion did not accept or include such practices. Israelite men engaged in such sex only when they violated their allegiance to Yahweh alone and worshiped other gods at Canaanite sanctuaries, or when Israelite religious leaders strayed from true Yahweh worship and allowed such practices to be introduced into Israelite sanctuaries. The idea that non-Israelite religions engaged in what were described as degrading sexual practices became so widely accepted that it appears in most introductory textbooks and Bible study guides.

In recent years, however, several scholars have reinvestigated this question. Most now agree that the category of "sacred prostitute" never existed either in Canaanite and Mesopotamian religions or in Israel. This reassessment marks a huge and dramatic shift in scholars' understanding of the similarities and differences between the religious practices of Israel and those of its neighbors.

Earlier scholars, it is now believed, wrongly generalized from a few allusions to sexual activity in temples found in texts from a much later period and a different geographical area. They also confused references to ordinary prostitutes who made themselves available in the neighborhoods near pilgrimage sites with references to female temple personnel. Female temple personnel did exist, but the new research shows that they were not involved in sexual activity.[1] Gomer could not have been a "sacred prostitute" because this category did not exist.

Which of the other two options is more likely? Was Gomer an ordinary prostitute, or was she engaged in nonpaid illicit sexual behavior? The answer depends on the meaning of the Hebrew word *zenunim*, which is used to describe Gomer in 1:2. The word *zenunim* is derived from the basic Hebrew root *znh*. (A "root" is the basic set of letters from which various nouns, verbs, and adjectives having related meanings are derived.) The general meaning of the verb *zanah* involves illicit sexual activity. It most often refers to sexual activity initiated by a woman that violates the rights of the man who is the guardian of her sexuality, usually her father if she is unmarried or her husband if she is married. Occasionally the verb is used to mean "to engage in prostitution," and the word for "prostitute" is *zonah*.[2]

But Gomer is not called *zonah*, or prostitute, a noun form indicating a profession, but instead is referred to as "a woman of *zenunim*," which is a different noun form that indicates "habitual behavior and inclination."[3] Thus it appears most likely that her behavior referred to in 1:2 was sex before marriage, but not professional prostitution.

The issue is not simple, of course, and in Hosea 2:5b, 12a we do find imagery that sounds like paid sex, hence prostitution:

> For she said, "I will go after my lovers;
> > they give me my bread and my water,
> > my wool and my flax, my oil and my drink."
> . . . . . . . . . . . . . . . . . . . . . . . . . . . . . . . . . . .
> I will lay waste her vines and her fig trees,
> > of which she said,

"These are my pay,
    which my lovers have given me."

These verses, however, occur in the midst of a lengthy and complex metaphorical poem in which the prophet is picturing the actions of the people of Israel, whom God accuses of trying to achieve greater material prosperity by worshiping other gods. There is not an exact analogy between Gomer and Israel in the metaphor, and so we do not learn something specific about Gomer herself from these verses. The evidence from the vocabulary of chapter 1 that she was not a prostitute remains convincing.

### 4. Why Are Gomer's Children Called "Children of Whoredom"?

Finally, what does it mean that Hosea should "have children of *zenunim*" (1:2)? It is clear from the biographical information in Hosea 1:3 that the children are conceived and born after Hosea marries Gomer. Is Hosea the father? Or does Gomer engage in promiscuous activity during her marriage as well as before it?

We cannot answer this question with certainty. On the one hand, the biographer says nothing explicit about the paternity question, and the phrase "bore him [Hosea] a son" in 1:3 strongly suggests that Hosea fathered at least the first child. On the other hand, if Gomer had violated her marriage relationship, her real life would be a better parallel for the long metaphorical poem about Israel as an unfaithful wife. The poem in Hosea 2 includes imagery of the rift between God and Israel ("she is not my wife, and I am not her husband," 2:2), and chapter 3 is usually understood as describing the prophet seeking out his wife despite the rift. Whether the rift was at Gomer's initiative with her lovers, or was Hosea's response to her behavior, it appears probable that Gomer engaged in illicit sexual behavior during the marriage.

As I suggested with regard to prostitution, however, the poetic metaphor in chapter 2 is multifaceted and greatly elaborated; the individual lines or phrases do not necessarily point to specific facts of Gomer's behavior. Because Hosea's marriage to a woman who was not a virgin was almost unthinkable in Israelite society, the stigma of her past behavior would follow her into her marriage. That stigma would probably extend to the children regardless of their actual paternity, so that the community may well have viewed Gomer's children as "children of whoredom" because of her past. In sum, Gomer may or may not have had sex with other men while married to Hosea; we cannot know for sure. Even if she did not, people may have assumed that she did.

### *A Word of Caution*

Although I assume that Gomer and her children were real people, and that Hosea married Gomer knowing that she was not a traditional Israelite virgin, it is important not to pretend that we have more than the barest sketch of their relationship. The purpose of the prophecy recorded for us is "not to give a complete account of his domestic tragedy and its outcome, but to speak to his people the word of Yahweh. His own experience is recorded, not for its own sake (and therefore not necessarily completely), but in order to express the enormity of Israel's apostasy, the reality of divine judgment, and possibility of restoration."[4]

### What Does Hosea Want to Teach Us about God?

Many readers have significant theological as well as personal objections to the fact that Hosea uses his relationship with Gomer as a vehicle for interpreting God's relationship with Israel. I discuss some of these difficulties in the next section. Despite these objections, I believe that Hosea accomplishes something important for our understanding of God that should not be overlooked or erased by the facts that his wife is used as an object lesson and that his message portrays women in a negative light.

Hosea uses the imagery of God as husband and Israel as wife to clarify and emphasize the personal character of the covenant relationship between God and Israel. While most of us tend today to think of God as tender, personal, and loving in relationship to us, this was not always the case. In Israel's early history, the principal imagery for the covenant relationship was primarily political rather than personal. It was Hosea who introduced the personal dimension.

Some background information about the concept of covenant will help to explain what is new in the book of Hosea. The Hebrew word *berith* refers to both religious covenants and political treaties and, in fact, has its roots in the secular world of formal, legal, political relationships. Ancient Israelites would have used this same word to describe both their relationship with God and, for example, the political deal between King Ahab and his rival Ben-Hadad of Damascus (1 Kgs. 20:34) or the arrangement between Israel and the powerful Assyrians on the march seeking control of Palestine (Hos. 12:1). A political overlord from a powerful land might make a treaty that promised caring, benevolent treatment of an obedient vassal (a small dependent nation), but the focus was on the political dimension. The overlord would simply punish a vassal who disobeyed; he would not experience any personal pain over the disobedience of the vassal or the measures he took in order to force compliance with his wishes.

In Israel before the time of Hosea, the religious covenant between God and Israel was understood primarily by analogy to such political treaties. When, in speaking of covenant, Hosea uses marriage imagery filled with language of intimacy and emotion, his prophecy introduces something new into this earlier political and formal view of God's relationship with Israel. Hosea gives expression to the deep relationship of care and tenderness that differentiates God and God's covenant with Israel from human political overlords and their human treaties. Although the political imagery of covenant continues, the marriage imagery allows Hosea to express God's anguish and frustration over the unfaithfulness of the human partner,[5] rather than just the uncaring, threatening vengefulness that a despotic political leader might pour out on a recalcitrant, rebellious, disloyal vassal.

The introduction of marriage imagery has additional consequences, as well. By portraying Israel as a faithless wife rather than a disobedient vassal, Hosea can introduce the imagery of multiple lovers and develop the metaphor of these lovers of the promiscuous Israel in a variety of ways. Clearly, the lovers represent those other than God with whom Israel is involved. Most often those others are other gods, but at some points, they are the other nations. In fact the other nations and other gods are related, because Israel's worship of other gods was sometimes associated with international political alliances. Solomon, for example, set up sanctuaries for the foreign wives he married to cement political alliances with his neighbors (1 Kgs. 11:7–8); and Ahab, who married Jezebel for political reasons, built a sanctuary for the god Baal, the chief god of her tradition (1 Kgs. 16:31–32). Thus it is not surprising that here in Hosea Israel's "lovers" can symbolize both foreign nations and foreign gods. In fact, in many cases the metaphor may point to both options at the same time.

Relying on the symbolic power of his marriage to Gomer, Hosea capitalizes on the emotional intimacy of marriage as well as the multifaceted symbolism of Israel's "lovers" to make five points about Israel and God that mutually inform one another:

1. Hosea uses his marriage to point to God's *undeserved election* of Israel. God chose to enter into relationship with Israel not because Israel was more powerful or more righteous or otherwise more desirable than any other people, but because God simply decided to do so. Similarly in Hosea's marriage as a prophetic acted sign, Hosea does not marry Gomer for any reason understandable from a human point of view. A promiscuous woman would not have been regarded as a desirable wife for any man in ancient Israel.

2. Hosea's marriage to Gomer also symbolizes Israel's *persistent apostasy, or faithlessness.* While the text is not completely clear about Gomer's behavior after her marriage to Hosea, it suggests that she was not faithful to Hosea, so that he separated from her.

3. The failure of the marriage and the threat or actuality of separation points to God's *rejection of or giving up on Israel*, the rupture of the covenant relationship expressed metaphorically in the phrase "she is not my wife, and I am not her husband" (2:2).

This idea, that the community could be so unfaithful that God would (even temporarily) abandon efforts to relate to the people, is an aspect of the Old Testament witness that most of us do not like to think about in relation to our own faith. It is certainly the case, in Hosea and in other traditions throughout the Old Testament, that God's mercy always outlasts God's anger. But just as some people today believe they are so bad that God has given up on them, so also the Israelites clearly believed that God could/would/ might give up on them, for this theme appears not just in Hosea, but also in Deuteronomy, Amos, Jeremiah, and other prophets. Challenging the idea that God had abandoned Israel forever is one of the primary themes of the prophecy in Isaiah 40–55. Perhaps today those of us who emphasize God's everlasting love and forgiveness need to beware of "cheap grace" that may tempt us to take too lightly the need for faithfulness and justice in our personal and communal lives.

4. In Hosea 2:9–10 the withholding of food and clothing and the apparent public ridicule of the unfaithful wife are symbolic of the *judgment* that God will bring upon the unfaithful community.

5. Finally, Hosea uses the story of the restoration of the marriage relationship (3:1–5; 2:14; 2:16) to symbolize God's initiative for the *purification and restoration* of the community of faith. Doom is not the last word that God calls Hosea to proclaim. There is hope beyond the judgment. God will initiate a new covenant involving all creation (2:18):

> "I will take you for my wife forever; I will take you for my wife in righteousness and in justice, in steadfast love, and in mercy. I will take you for my wife in faithfulness; and you shall know the LORD." (2:19–20)

Since the people are apparently unable to achieve proper covenant living on their own, God will give them the gifts they need as wedding presents: righteousness, justice, steadfast love, mercy, and faithfulness, so that a right relationship between God and

God's people can be achieved. It is an incredible promise, still good today: God commits to us even in the midst of our sin and failure; and God still offers those same gifts, empowering us individually and together in community to live faithfully in relation to God and neighbor.

## Dangerous Imagery?

Despite the power of Hosea's message and the effectiveness of his marriage metaphor in portraying God's anguish over the unfaithfulness of the people, the metaphor presents us also with a serious problem, one developed most fully by womanist scholar Renita Weems, particularly in her book *Battered Love*.[6] The husband who expresses anguish nonetheless uses his power to punish the unfaithful wife. Weems suggests that the effectiveness of Hosea's metaphor for the relationship between Israel and God depends upon three basic cultural assumptions about marriage:

1. In a marriage relationship the husband holds power and control; the wife is dependent upon him and subordinate to him.
2. Trouble in a marriage is generally the wife's fault, whether she has engaged in illicit sex or not.
3. It is therefore the prerogative and perhaps even the duty of the husband to do whatever he can to correct a wayward wife.[7]

And we may add a fourth assumption, concerning prostitution: Hosea's metaphorical representation of Israel as a prostitute (2:7, 13) is effective only if prostitution is understood as a behavior freely chosen by the woman.

These four cultural assumptions were deeply embedded in ancient Israelite thought. Although many people explicitly reject them in our own culture today, I would argue that they still remain powerful undercurrents in our thinking. Most of us know at an intellectual level that statistically husbands commit adultery more than wives, and that globally prostitution is linked to kidnapping, lockups, inescapable poverty, and international Mafia-like cartels. Nevertheless, we are not always conscious of how deeply the biblical imagery of illicit sex and prostitution here in Hosea, as well as in Jeremiah and Ezekiel, can undercut women's understanding of their identity as persons made in the image of God. The story of Gomer and of the divine husband's punishment of his disobedient wife Israel can all too easily (even if not consciously) become a basis for human husbands' treatment of wives whose actions displease them.

The imagery for God's judgment of Israel within Hosea's marriage metaphor is particularly difficult and dangerous. Hosea 2 tells us that the divine husband will restrict his wife's movements:

> "I will hedge up her way with thorns; and I will build a wall against her." (2:6)

He will control her financially:

> "I will lay waste her vines and her fig trees." (v. 12)

He will withhold food and drink:

> "I will . . . make her like a wilderness, and turn her into a parched land, and kill her with thirst." (v. 3)

> "I will take back my grain in its time, and my wine in its season." (v. 9)

He will "strip her naked and expose her as in the day she was born" (v. 3); he will "punish her" (v. 13), and he will have "no pity" on her children (v. 4).

In recent years women's advocacy groups and the media have helped us to become more informed about the behavior patterns of abusive husbands. As public awareness has grown, shelters for battered women have been established in cities and towns all across the country. Hosea's metaphorical description of Israel's punishment as the punishment to be meted out to a wife whose actions displease her husband fits the pattern of abusive situations all too well—physical restriction, deprivation of basic necessities, humiliation and threats. If this is Hosea's description of how God will treat Israel, may he have treated his wife Gomer in the same way? The marriage as a prophetic acted sign was intended to show the people their own unfaithfulness, but it might also have been used to show how God would respond. It is a chilling possibility. The divine husband concludes his scathing condemnation in v. 13:

> I will punish her for the festival days of the Baals,
>     when she offered incense to them
> and decked herself with her ring and jewelry,
>     and went after her lovers,
>     and forgot me, says the LORD.

But immediately his mood changes and chapter 2 continues with the marvelous vision of restoration and reunion I noted earlier among the important themes of Hosea's message:

> Therefore, I will now allure her,
>     and bring her into the wilderness,
>     and speak tenderly to her.
> 
> (2:14)

Once we have recognized the language of spousal battering, however, even this beautiful restoration imagery may leave us a little ill at ease; for this change of tone is reminiscent of what counselors have come to identify as a typical pattern of an abusive husband who, after a period of renewed tenderness, will return to his abusive ways. In Hosea, of course, the theological picture is of the end time, when God will renew all creation and a right relationship will prevail "forever" (2:18–19). At the level of human relationships between husbands and wives, however, we know that such promises of "forever" are not so reliable.

One response to this analysis of Hosea's imagery is just not to take it seriously. We may think to ourselves that God is good, God is not really abusive; Hosea's words are "only imagery." We know that God is not fickle like an abusive husband, and furthermore, we believe that whatever sins we have committed are forgiven in Christ, so that we will not experience divine judgment.

Yes, at one level Hosea's words are "only imagery." Nonetheless, the images are still dangerous. The statistics about battered women suggest that every community still includes men who believe their word is law, enforceable by violence in their own homes, and women whose husbands exercise such power over them. If we lift up only the positive imagery of tenderness and restoration in Hosea, and do not challenge the negative aspects with which we disagree, we may unintentionally allow both batterers and victims to believe that these biblical verses justify such behavior.

This problem is not restricted to interpreting Hosea. The traditional and still much used New Testament imagery of the church as bride of Christ has its roots precisely in this Hosea tradition. When we speak of the church as bride of Christ and of Christ's love for the church, and in that context speak of the waywardness of the church, which the Lord of the church will discipline in order to purify and renew, we reiterate the same paradigm that we find in the marriage imagery of Hosea. It is true, and thankfully so, that we do not use Hosea's graphic imagery of battering to describe God's purifying and renewing action. Nonetheless, I urge caution in using marriage imagery to speak about God. Perhaps we need not abandon this metaphor; but we need to be more explicit about which aspects of the comparison are significant and which we should discount or reject as inappropriate.

## Concluding Reflection

In conclusion, I ask you to reflect on Hosea's use of his family situation as a public example for his prophesying. Given the content of his prophecy, I cannot imagine any woman who would have wanted to be Gomer. No matter what a woman had done wrong, she would not want to be subjected to such public humiliation, used by her husband as an object lesson in her own community to make a point about God.

As we consider the situation from Gomer's point of view and sympathize with her plight, we may wonder whether there was another side to a story. We think we know who Gomer was because Hosea has presented her to us in a certain way. As we have seen in previous chapters, however, authors of biblical books have their own particular concerns, and those concerns affect how they present women to us. Perhaps Gomer would tell us a different story. Mary Caroline Jonah offers one possibility for Gomer's side of the story in her poem "The Autobiography of Gomer." The poem follows the basic sequence of relationships mentioned in the biblical text, but gives us a very different perspective on them.

The Autobiography of Gomer
Mary Caroline Jonah

Gomer.
That's me, that's what they call me.
Gomer
the whore.
For 2500 years men have told their women about
Gomer
the whore.
Bitter?
I'm not bitter.
It's just that after 2600 years of being
Gomer
the whore,
how else am I to talk to people?
I've no privacy.
Everybody knows who Gomer is.
And they all know what I am!
If everybody knows you are, you might as well be.

Gomer.
I wasn't always like this.
Once I was young and free
And I danced and ran in the breeze on the hills

And my hair streamed out behind me
And I swung it around and around my head like a bucket on a
    string.
And I sang in the wind
So the birds answered my call.
Once I was young.
And one came and danced with me.
Oh, he was fair, graceful and strong as a hind.
Gazelles we were, flowing together in the sunlight.
Did we Do It?
What difference does it make?
If everybody knows you did, you might as well have
    done it.

Gomer
And her lover.
Well, they caught us.
Or me, rather—
He got away.
Go, my love, I'd rather one of us got free
Than both of us in chains for
2700 years or so.
They were going to stone me—
All those men with stones in their hands.
My friends—Jehu, Nathan, Obed—
When I was younger, we danced together on the hill.
Now they stood there hating me.
If everyone says you are, you might as well be.

Gomer
the whore.
Then this strange man came out of nowhere,
With his hair in strings and dirt in his ears
And he yelled, Stop
And they stopped.
Can you imagine, they stopped!

With all that noise, and all that hate,
they stopped.
And he bought me from my father,
my father standing there with a stone
in his hand, hate in his eyes, and tears on his cheeks.
He said he wanted to marry this whore,
That God had sent him to marry this whore.
If they're sure you are, you might as well be.

Gomer
the whore.
So my father sold me to him
For two pieces of silver and a kid with a lame leg.
And they took us to the priest and he married us,
Me and that strange man with his hair in strings.
And he took me to his home, and he knew me.
Can you imagine, he thought he knew me!
Strange man, you don't learn to know anybody
That way.
He knew me, and now I wasn't a whore
because I was a wife now, and a wife isn't a whore
if she stops with her husband.
Yahweh!
Listen to me, I haven't called you for a millennium
Or two.
Listen to me Yahweh, you unnameable God of men,
and answer me:
You never asked me if I wanted that man,
You two just used me to teach a lesson.
Answer me, Yahweh:
My father bought my life with my body.
When was I a whore,
When I danced free on the hill with a man like a gazelle,
Or when I lay in bed with a man who
Bought my body to teach Israel a lesson?
If everybody knows which it was, it might as well have been.

Gomer
the whore.
He called Israel Gomer after me:
Gomer
the whore
Israel
the whore.
I guess that makes me Israel.
Did you ever think of yourself as a country?
Let's see, I guess Jerusalem's over here, and—
That's silly, the mountains are in quite the wrong place!
Did you ever think of yourself as a lesson?
I guess I'm a strange lesson to teach anyone.
Strange man, are you sure you want Israel to learn that
    lesson?
Maybe they'll end up feeling like me:
If everyone calls you one, you might as well be.

Gomer
the whore.
So he knew me, he says, and I had a baby.
"God Sows," he called it.
Strange man, you sowed it. I know who's been sowing in
    my field.
And I was being a wife, then.
Or perhaps you had something else in mind.
A strange fruit Yahweh sows.
A strange lesson for Israel.
That wasn't enough, I had another baby.
This one he calls, "Not Loved"!
"Not Loved," did you ever hear of such a thing?
A baby, "Not Loved"!
Strange man, did you ever ask me?
Did you ever once ask me what I wanted to name my
    baby?
"Not Loved," you called my lovely, my little one.
If that's what you call us, that's what we must be.

Gomer and her babies
Not loved.
God sowed again. Or that man did,
it doesn't matter now, but I was still being a wife.
God sowed, and there was another baby.
This time he disowned us all.
"Not My People."
Not my people. I knew it all the time.
Who would call his wife a whore and be one person with her,
the way Adam was with Eve?
Before I thought, now I know.
Not my people,
So I went away.
Not right away, of course. I took my time.
But one day, when the moon was full,
And the breeze was soft on the hill,
I went.
If everyone knows you don't belong, you might as well go.

Gomer and her babies
Not my people.
Oh, great and terrible Lord, whose people are we?
Do you think I worship Astarte, and sacrifice to the Asherah?
They say even the Egyptians are your people, the Cushites.
Whose people are we?
So we went away.
I looked for the young man I remembered,
my graceful hind.
But the hills were empty.
So I found a man who was kind to us,
Who never shamed us in front of the people
Or called us names.
And we lived with him.
They say I was unfaithful.
How can you be unfaithful to someone
who calls you "Not my people"?
Who was unfaithful to whom?

Oh, well.
If everyone knows you're wrong, you might as well be.

Gomer
the unfaithful.
But I was faithful to the man who took us in.
And then one day *he* came along.
He didn't speak to me, just looked and passed me by,
Spitting a little through his teeth.
"I want her back," he said to the man who was kind to us.
"She's my wife. I'll take you to the city gates if you keep her."
"If you let her come, I'll pay you for her. She's cost you money."
Then I spoke up, I who had never spoken before,
I who had been silent, as a good wife should,
Until life and time spit me out, like vomit, upon the earth.
"I won't come," I said.
"I won't come back to someone who will call us
Not My People.
I won't come back to someone who
calls us Not Loved.
These are our names: Woman Bears,
Beloved,
and My People.
Call us by our names. Then we will return."
"You are right," he said. "Those are your names, though the
    eldest
is both Woman Bears and God Sows.
You are Beloved, and you are My People."
So we returned.
And I thought maybe I had a chance.
If nobody thinks about you, maybe you can be yourself.

Gomer.
Woman.
But it didn't happen.
Our people turned farther and farther from Yahweh.
He watched, while Yahweh's message burned in anguish in
    his bowels.

I watched, too, in anguish.
But my anguish was hard, cold fear:
Oh, my people, Israel. Do not rebel.
I do not want to be exposed again.
But time came, and he could not keep silent longer.
He snatched out the old words and hurled them at people
    again and again.
He sang out new words, sweeter than honey,
dripping with the pain of our lives.
"Return, my people! Return,
I am seeking after you as my prophet sought after Gomer.
I will take you back, and no more will you be unfaithful."
Remember Gomer, the unfaithful, and return.
Once more, this time never to cease,
My name was heard throughout the land.
Gomer
the unfaithful
Gomer
the whore.
If they know you are through all the ages, you might as
    well be.
Gomer
the unfaithful
Gomer
the unchangeable,
the eternal,
unredeemable
whore.

Once there was a man—
I never met him, but I watched him a long time.
He wouldn't have called me a whore,
he never talked to women that way
And he didn't think much of stoning people either.
I was almost beginning to trust him
when they killed him.
But I guess I was wrong about him
Because his followers right away started talking about me—

Gomer
the whore
Gomer
the whore.
If they're going to talk about you that way you might as well
    be that way . . .

Gomer
the whore.
But there's one thing I know:
He never called any woman a whore![8]

## Questions for Personal Reflection and Group Study

1. Readers have very different (and often very strong) reactions to the poem that concludes this chapter. List some adjectives that describe your response. What factors such as your view of the Bible or your awareness of women's struggles affect your response?
2. Which picture of Gomer is more meaningful to you personally, the traditional picture or the picture in the poem? Why? What may be lost and what may be gained by thinking of Gomer in such different ways?
3. Study the poem alongside Hosea 1–3. Try to discern how the sequence of events in the poem parallels the movement in the biblical text.
4. Do you tend to think of God more like a distant ruler or more like a close family member? What imagery would you use to describe God's reaction when you do something wrong?
5. Through Hosea's prophecy God promises to empower the community to live a more faithful life. What does your community most need from God right now? What do you need individually?
6. What is your view of Israel's cultural assumptions about marriage listed in the chapter? Do you know people who hold a different opinion? How do you think these assumptions affect our society today?

7. What is happening in support of battered women in your community? In what ways is your congregation (or other churches) involved?

## Notes

1. For a discussion of such confusion in the interpretation of Hos. 4:13–14, see Phyllis Bird, "'To Play the Harlot': An Inquiry into an Old Testament Metaphor," in *Gender and Difference in Ancient Israel* (ed. Peggy L. Day; Minneapolis: Fortress Press, 1989), 75–94.
2. Ibid., 76–79.
3. Ibid., 80.
4. G. W. Anderson, "Hosea and Yahweh: God's Love Story," *Review and Expositor* 72, no. 4 (1975): 425.
5. For more on this concept, see Abraham Heschel, *The Prophets* (New York: Harper & Row, 1962), 489–92.
6. Renita J. Weems, *Battered Love: Marriage, Sex, and Violence in the Hebrew Prophets* (Minneapolis: Fortress Press, 1995).
7. Ibid., 18–19.
8. Mary Caroline Jonah, "The Autobiography of Gomer," unpublished poem, 1975. Used by permission.

*Chapter Six*

# The Good Wife:
# Who *Is* a Worthy Woman?
## Proverbs 31:10–31

The concluding passage of the book of Proverbs has been given various names: "the good wife," "ode to a capable wife," "in praise of a worthy woman." People often recognize the first line, even if they don't know that the words are from the Bible:

> A capable wife who can find?
> She is far more precious than jewels.
> (Prov. 31:10)

In Hebrew, this text is an alphabetical acrostic poem, in which each line of the poem begins with the next letter of the alphabet. (Naturally this feature of the poem cannot be seen in English translation.) As is the case with other acrostic poems in the Old Testament, the acrostic feature tends to eliminate tight organizational direction or systematic thematic progress through the poem, so the poem cannot be readily summarized, and different readers tend to highlight different ideas found in it.

The poem is sometimes described as advice to young Israelite men about what kind of wife to look for, and sometimes as advice to young Israelite girls about how they should aspire to live out their anticipated future as married women. As advice instilled in young people of ancient Israel—men and women—about the qualities of a good wife, the poem would continue to influence their expectations after they were married. And the poem continues to have its impact on expectations for marriage even today. As part of our biblical canon, it contributes to people's views of what makes a good wife—its words may indeed be more influential in some Christian communities today than they were in the biblical period, when the text was known mostly in court circles and did not have sacred status as "word of God."

Over the years I have asked students about their associations in memory and experience with this passage. I have learned that in many congregations this passage is regularly read and interpreted in church on Mother's Day Sunday morning. Although I have heard this use mentioned proportionately more frequently by African-Americans and by Christians from non-Western congregations, it is also traditional in many white North American congregations. Other students have reported that this text was read at their mother's wedding or at the funeral of an aunt or grandmother. One woman knew the text as a gift from a friend—a needlepoint framed for a wall hanging given as a present when she was expecting her first child. Others have heard the text used at a wedding anniversary celebration. Many cherish this passage deeply, while others raise questions about its value.

## The Biblical Text

A capable wife who can find?
　　She is far more precious than jewels.
The heart of her husband trusts in her,
　　and he will have no lack of gain.
She does him good, and not harm,
　　all the days of her life.
She seeks wool and flax,
　　and works with willing hands.
She is like the ships of the merchant,
　　she brings her food from far away.

She rises while it is still night
  and provides food for her household
  and tasks for her servant girls.
She considers a field and buys it;
  with the fruit of her hands she plants a vineyard.
She girds herself with strength,
  and makes her arms strong.
She perceives that her merchandise is profitable.
  Her lamp does not go out at night.
She puts her hands to the distaff,
  and her hands hold the spindle.
She opens her hand to the poor,
  and reaches out her hands to the needy.
She is not afraid for her household when it snows,
  for all her household are clothed in crimson.
She makes herself coverings;
  her clothing is fine linen and purple.
Her husband is known in the city gates,
  taking his seat among the elders of the land.
She makes linen garments and sells them;
  she supplies the merchant with sashes.
Strength and dignity are her clothing,
  and she laughs at the time to come.
She opens her mouth with wisdom,
  and the teaching of kindness is on her tongue.
She looks well to the ways of her household,
  and does not eat the bread of idleness.
Her children rise up and call her happy;
  her husband too, and he praises her:
"Many women have done excellently,
  but you surpass them all."
Charm is deceitful, and beauty is vain,
  but a woman who fears the LORD is to be praised.
Give her a share in the fruit of her hands,
  and let her works praise her in the city gates.
                                   (Prov. 31:10–31)

## Voices of North American Readers

During the years in which I've taught this poem, many North American women have described their own reactions to and interpretations of it. Their responses most often fall into five points of view or perspectives, which I share below. Imagine you are listening in on a women's Bible study group, as the members explain their points of view. I hope you will sense something of the mood as well as the content of each viewpoint. As you read, try to imagine the contemporary women who read the text in these different ways, and try to make your first reaction one of empathy with each interpretation, however far it may be from your own understanding of the text or experience of it. I hope you will be able to stand for a moment in the shoes of women whose viewpoints or life experiences are very different from your own.

### Reader 1: Beyond Tradition

For me this text offers a new horizon of freedom for women, an open door through which women can move out of and beyond traditional stereotypes of their role in Western society. Notice how the text portrays a woman involved in economic transactions: "she considers a field and buys it" (v. 16). She may be a business-woman—"She perceives that her merchandise is profitable" (v. 18); "She makes linen garments and sells them" (v. 24a); "she supplies the merchant with sashes" (v. 24b). In short, she's a capable woman who does many things outside the home.

My family and my community think women should concentrate just on taking care of children, cooking a good meal, and being active in the church, and I find that frustrating. For me, reading this passage validates my desire to work outside the home, to do something more beyond family and church.

I've learned that the Hebrew word translated "wife" (v. 10) can also mean "woman," without regard for marital status. So perhaps this text offers a model for the life of unmarried women as well; only a few of the verses refer explicitly to a husband or children. Maybe women who are single—by choice or by "chance"—are praised here for their talents and abilities—that's a theme sadly overlooked in most of the Old Testament. This woman's talents include not just economic employment, but wise speaking, inner strength, and concern for the needy, and all of these can be exhibited by single women as well as married women. So for me this passage connects the concerns of women in two very different circumstances: married women severely confined to traditional household roles who dream of expanding the horizons of their responsibilities and opportunities, and single women who feel the Bible ignores them. In this passage, they can both find a basis for valuing work outside the home.

### Reader 2: Economic Status

It seems to me that this text concentrates on praising the behavior of a wealthy married woman. The fact that she is involved in economic transactions may not be sufficient to make my point, because of course women of all socioeconomic classes, whether rich or poor, can participate in this kind of buying and selling. But the references to fabrics of fine linen, with crimson and purple dyes (vv. 21, 22, 24), the most expensive of the ancient world, point in the direction of a wealthy household.

I think my interpretation is confirmed by the references to "servant girls" (v. 15) and the purchase of a field (v. 16). In my opinion, the woman's care for the poor and needy (v. 20) sounds like a rich person's "handout" to the less fortunate. That's commendable behavior but not necessarily a difficult or sacrificial action. For me, her wealth is confirmed by her husband's status as he takes his seat among the elders at the city gates (v. 23); that's the place where prominent citizens met to decide judicial cases and other community matters. In the ending of the story of Ruth, for example, the prominent and wealthy citizen Boaz spoke at the city gate with the next-of-kin in the presence of the Bethlehem elders.

I don't think the poem explains whether this woman is wealthy because she married into wealth, or because she was herself from a wealthy family and brought a good dowry to her marriage, or because she herself works. Whichever the case, if this is the model for the praiseworthy woman, very few could ever attain praise. There are very few rich men, fewer wealthy girls, and equally few who could work successfully enough to get as rich as this family appears to be. If this poem describes the kind of wife a man should seek to marry, then everybody loses, because it presumes a fairy-tale world; it denigrates ordinary women without a lot of money and by implication their ordinary husbands as well.

### Reader 3: All for Husband and Family

I think this passage implies that there is only one approved option women can desire or hope for—a family-centered life. Only married women are praised here, and everything for which wives are praised is connected to home life. There is no life envisioned for them beyond their household duties. Although I wish I could find the nontraditional themes suggested by the first reader, I just can't read it that way.

As I see it, the text begins with "capable wife" (v. 10), immediately moves to her relationship with her husband, who can trust her and who does well economically ("no lack of gain") because of her (v. 11). She does him good, not harm (v. 12), and this might even imply that many or most wives do harm to their husbands, since this truly capable wife is so hard to find (v. 10). None of her work beyond the walls of her home is done for its own sake or represents any independent "career." Rather, all her efforts are directly connected to providing food and clothing for her family: she rises while it is still night to provide food (v. 15), apparently getting up early to start the cooking. After she buys a field, she herself plants the vineyard. She spins and weaves and dyes clothing, and sells the surplus. But all of these outside buying and selling activities are strictly a part of her ordinary household responsibilities. She is never idle in looking after her household (v. 27), so both her children and her husband praise her. Her appreciative husband will rightly say, "Many women have done excellently, but you surpass them all" (v. 29).

We *should* honor stay-at-home moms as much as career women, and this text is great for showing how hard it is to be a full-time mother. But since the Hebrew words for "woman" and "wife" are the same, I think the text tells women and men that all women ought to get married and stay at home raising a family. It says nothing to support the idea of women having careers.

### Reader 4: Building the Husband's Reputation

I think this passage praises the wife primarily because of the glory she can bring to her husband. After all, it's the husband who is interested in having such a wife; no one is asking the woman what she thinks about this portrait of herself. He can trust her, will have no lack of gain; she does him good, not harm. It is her industriousness and financial acumen that contribute to the growing wealth of the family. She's the one recognized in the community for her magnanimity to the needy and those less well off. She's the one who speaks wisely and fears God.

Not that there's anything wrong with all these attributes; I'd like to have them myself. But the woman seems to be viewed only as a means to improving her husband's life and his standing in the community. The passage is definitely written from a man's point of view. Because of her behavior her husband has a prominent reputation and a seat in the deliberations at the city gates (v. 23). The goal of having such a wife is that "her works praise her in the city gates" (v. 31), where the men sit and between moments of business compare notes about their wives. I fear that her husband would be urging her to do more and more so that he could out-brag his friends about his wonderful wife.

### Reader 5: This Is Supermom

From my point of view, this text is the perfect description—or prescription—for a superwoman or supermom. Here is a picture of a woman who can do everything, who never needs any sleep ("Her lamp does not go out at night," v. 18), who can be merchant, farmer, seamstress, chef, organizer, fountain of wisdom, volunteer worker, who has perfect children who bless her rather than whine or fight, and who can see to her husband's advancement.

I don't think any real-life mother could possibly live up to what is pictured here. No woman can feel good about herself so long as she measures herself by a standard that cannot be attained. But this text, and in my opinion our culture as well, urges all women to strive toward this unattainable goal.

On the other hand, the one thing the text does not require is charm and physical beauty. In verse 30 these are explicitly set aside in favor of fearing, or showing reverence for, the Lord. In our modern Western culture, of course, physical beauty is normally high on the list of features that women strive for. And so many women assume that beauty can't be achieved without expensive cosmetics, sexy underwear, luxurious bath soap, Botox injections, or plastic surgery. This point in verse 30 about downplaying physical appearance might be a comfort to many women, but it has been fairly successfully undercut in our society by the advertising campaigns from the manufacturers of beauty products.

And so our imaginary North American Bible study draws to a close. What a remarkable variety of interpretations the readers have set before us! But the possibilities are not ended, as we see when we turn to an interpretation from another cultural setting.

### A Southern African Reading

Madipoane Masenya, a Northern Sotho woman in the context of South Africa, shows that many of the same perspectives voiced by North American women can also be found in a very different context.[1] The cultural context in which Masenya develops her interpretation is complicated. The Northern Sotho and other African peoples had their own strong cultural traditions and customs for centuries before the European colonization of Africa. The economic structures and the religious and cultural traditions brought by the Europeans caused great change and upheaval in the traditional African societies. Although many of the old values are still appreciated by African peoples today, it is sometimes difficult to implement them in the new environment or circumstances in which they live. Masenya interprets the poem from Proverbs in a way that attempts to take seriously both the strengths and the limitations of traditional African culture. As she does this, she seeks to walk a fine line between unthinking praise and unthinking rejection of the features of Western culture that came to Africa with missionaries and traders.

One cultural difference of particular importance for interpreting the poem has to do with spheres of work inside and outside the home. Western culture developed this distinction mainly after the industrial revolution, when the so-called public sphere of work outside the home (done mostly by men) came to be valued more highly than the so-called private sphere of caring for the home and children (done mostly by women). This division of labor is basic to the views of the first and third North American readers, but, as Masenya notes, it did not exist in traditional African culture but was introduced by the Western colonizers.

Masenya acknowledges that the poem about the good wife presents an unattainable ideal, an ideal that serves the interests of men and presumes an upper-class woman. Thus far she concurs with the views of North American readers 2, 4, and 5. But these facts, she argues, do not automatically render the text oppressive to poor Northern Sotho women. In her cultural context, for instance, many poor women function for all practical purposes as heads of household, because Western capitalist employment structures and the continuing legacy of apartheid policies have forced their husbands to seek work in distant cities. For such women Masenya affirms the role of household manager as a potential position of power appreciated by the text. She also lifts up caring for the needy (v. 20) and being hardworking (vv. 13, 15, 19) as basic values for women of Northern Sotho culture, while at the same time arguing that her culture rightly expects these qualities as much from men as from women. Even those who are not wealthy are called to care for the less fortunate.

Masenya's principal concern for the negative impact of Proverbs 31 upon women in her culture is its presumption of the traditional family model of husband, wife, and children. This text will not be liberating, she says, for women in her culture who are not in traditional family configurations, for by implication it denigrates or at least offers no guidance and encouragement for single mothers or women who remain part of extended family structures typical of traditional African culture. Here Masenya expands our interpretive horizons, as she lifts up new categories of women not previously addressed by the North American readers.

### Dealing with Diversity

The variety of approaches to Proverbs 31:10–31 in North America and elsewhere suggests that we must exercise care and respect in any discussion of it. When women who have found their purpose in life through this text encounter women for whom the text seems to say nothing, or even seems to denigrate their situations, whether they are childless, or unmarried, or single mothers, or poor, it can be painful to hear one another's different reactions. Some married women are glad to have a high standard set out for them, while others find themselves burdened by an unattainable goal, even while striving toward it and listening for every crumb of praise that tells them they are on the track toward it. Perhaps this passage is best used as a conversation opener about how women understand their own identity, rather than as a prescription to be simply followed or rejected.

### Too Good to Be True?
### The Good Wife in Old Testament Narrative

If we look to narratives in the Old Testament for women who approximate this ideal, few if any women seem to measure up. Perhaps this is because such a perfect woman would not make very good narrative copy. Perhaps it is because such a woman is truly rare, as the text claims (v. 10). Among the women we have considered in this book, for example, we have few candidates. Hagar is a slave with no standing to act as the women in the poem, Sarah is cruel to Hagar, Gomer is portrayed as unfaithful, and Michal and Vashti insult their husbands. Esther speaks wisely, but we do not see her managing a household—everything is provided. We do not know any details of Naomi's relation to her husband Elimelech, and what we know of Bathsheba is not very pertinent to the categories of the Proverbs passage—except that she is beautiful, which Proverbs declares unimportant. Of the list, we are left with Ruth and Abigail as possible examples of the rare woman described by the author.

We don't know much about Ruth in her role as wife either of Boaz or of Naomi's dead son. Boaz is certainly impressed, however, with her behavior toward Naomi:

> All that you have done for your mother-in-law since the death of your husband has been fully told me, and how you left your father and mother and your native land and came to a people that you did not know before. May the LORD reward you for your deeds. (Ruth 2:11–12)

And he is also appreciative of her behavior in approaching him at the threshing floor:

> "May you be blessed by the LORD . . . you have not gone after young men, whether poor or rich." (Ruth 3:10)

Ruth's actions on Naomi's behalf fit many of the qualities of the good wife portrayed in Proverbs 31. She provides a basis for trust (Prov. 31:11), does good, not harm (v. 12), commits herself for "all the days of her life" (v. 12), "works with willing hands" (v. 13), expresses her willingness to reverence (fear) the God of Naomi (v. 30), shows "strength and dignity" (v. 25). Yet, Ruth is also desperately poor, and of course the evidence of her wifely qualities is shown toward her mother-in-law, rather than her husband. These are major differences. Yet, the spirit of Ruth certainly comports with the tone of Proverbs 31. And perhaps her behavior led Boaz to view her as a wonderful prospect for becoming for him "the good wife."

Abigail also embodies many characteristics of the ideal wife in Proverbs.[2] Although Abigail's husband is a "fool," she exercises prudence, a characteristic associated with wisdom. She is certainly wealthy; her husband is described as a wealthy man (1 Sam. 25:2), and she brings to David 200 loaves, 2 skins of wine, 5 dressed sheep, 5 measures of parched grain, 100 clusters of raisins, and 200 cakes of figs (v. 18). She speaks to David with wisdom and kindness (Prov. 31:26). Abigail uses both her wealth and her words wisely in order to defuse David's anger and thereby to save her husband and his workers. Her speech to David predicting his future certainly manifests her fear of (reverence for) the Lord (Prov. 31:30).

In chapter 4 I noted the difficulty of ascertaining Abigail's motives. Did she use her beauty and cleverness (1 Sam. 25:3) wisely to save her husband's household and prevent bloodshed, or as a scheme to change her personal life? Whatever her motives, probably most men as well as women would approve of her action once it turns out successfully. In the end she certainly has a better husband, at least from the viewpoint of the narrator. But the poem in Proverbs imagines neither a foolish husband nor a wife who undercuts her husband's decisions. So even Abigail relates only imperfectly to the Proverbs portrait of the capable wife.

### The Good Wife and Wisdom Woman

In the face of the humanly unattainable ideal in Proverbs 31, several scholars, particularly Kathleen O'Connor, have suggested another way to read the passage.[3] To grasp this approach, we must first step back from the assumption that the text is about human wives. When we move away from this literal meaning, the theme of Wisdom Woman, found in the book of Proverbs as a whole and especially in Proverbs 1–9, fairly pops into view as an alternative focus. As O'Connor puts it, "Drawing from images of the young man choosing between the Wisdom Woman or the Strange Woman found in Proverbs 1–9, this poem [chap. 31] demonstrates what life is like once one has chosen to live with the Wisdom Woman. . . . The benefits of life with [this woman] . . . are precisely the gifts that Wisdom Woman offers to those who seek her."[4]

The author of Proverbs 1–9 personifies wisdom and folly as two contrasting female characters, one of whom is everything good, valuable, and profitable for right living, while the other is in effect the path that leads to destruction. Each of these personified women calls out to men from the street corners, and the author urges that people (in his context he is actually thinking of men) use their best efforts not to be fooled by Woman Folly (also called the Strange Woman, and referred to as loose or adulterous), but to make the right choice and attach themselves to Woman Wisdom.

These images of wisdom and folly early in Proverbs are a creation of the male imagination, as is the woman of the poem in Proverbs 31. The danger of the figures of Woman Wisdom and Woman Folly is that they can reinforce the stereotypical female gender alternatives of "Madonna or whore," which leave no room for real, ordinary women and can have a damaging effect on women's self-image. O'Connor argues, however, that this negative stereotyping should not become the last word about Woman Wisdom, for Wisdom offers a life filled with hope, abundance, and peace for our troubled world.[5]

In Proverbs, Wisdom Woman becomes a character who acts and speaks, much as a character in narrative. Her speech, recorded in Proverbs 8, shows both the connections to Proverbs 31 and her importance:

> To you, O people, I call,
>> and my cry is to all that live.
> O simple ones, learn prudence;
>> acquire intelligence, you who lack it.
> Hear, for I will speak noble things,
>> and from my lips will come what is right;
> for my mouth will utter truth;
>> wickedness is an abomination to my lips.
> All the words of my mouth are righteous;
>> there is nothing twisted or crooked in them.
> They are all straight to one who understands
>> and right to those who find knowledge.
> Take my instruction instead of silver,
>> and knowledge rather than choice gold;
> for wisdom is better than jewels,
>> and all that you may desire cannot compare with her.

I, wisdom, live with prudence,
    and I attain knowledge and discretion.
The fear of the LORD is hatred of evil.
Pride and arrogance and the way of evil
    and perverted speech I hate.
I have good advice and sound wisdom;
    I have insight, I have strength.
By me kings reign,
    and rulers decree what is just;
by me rulers rule,
    and nobles, all who govern rightly.
I love those who love me,
    and those who seek me diligently find me.
Riches and honor are with me,
    enduring wealth and prosperity.
My fruit is better than gold, even fine gold,
    and my yield than choice silver.
I walk in the way of righteousness,
    along the paths of justice,
endowing with wealth those who love me,
    and filling their treasuries.

(Prov. 8:4–21)

In this passage Wisdom Woman describes herself and her gifts in themes strikingly reminiscent of the description of the good wife in Proverbs 31. She offers intelligence and prudence to all who will accept her gifts (8:4–5), says that she will speak what is right and true (vv. 6–7), and urges her hearers to accept her instruction, the content of wisdom, "for wisdom is better than jewels, and all you may desire cannot compare with her" (v. 11). She instills "the fear of the LORD" (v. 13), she has strength (v. 14), and with her are riches, honor, enduring wealth, and prosperity (v. 18). She endows with wealth those who love her (v. 21).

Who is this Wisdom Woman, then, who is not a human woman but who offers what one should desire in the ideal relationship? In Proverbs 8:22–31 Wisdom describes herself as one who existed with God "at the beginning" (v. 22).

The LORD created me at the beginning of his work,
  the first of his acts of long ago.
Ages ago I was set up,
  at the first, before the beginning of the earth.
When there were no depths I was brought forth,
  when there were no springs abounding with water.
Before the mountains had been shaped,
  before the hills, I was brought forth —
when he had not yet made earth and fields,
  or the world's first bits of soil.
When he established the heavens, I was there,
  when he drew a circle on the face of the deep,
when he made firm the skies above,
  when he established the fountains of the deep,
when he assigned to the sea its limit,
  so that the waters might not transgress his command,
when he marked out the foundations of the earth,
  then I was beside him, like a master worker;
and I was daily his delight,
  rejoicing before him always,
rejoicing in his inhabited world
  and delighting in the human race.

(Prov. 8:22–31)

This passage presents Wisdom Woman as with God before the beginning of creation (vv. 23–26) and participating with God in the creation of the world (vv. 27, 30). It holds in tension two ways of thinking about Wisdom's relation to God. On the one hand, wisdom is an essential attribute of God, part and parcel of the very being of God. God who is wise is God the Creator. On the other hand, the text also describes Wisdom as a close companion of God, or what is called a "hypostasis," a separate being intimately connected to and identified with God. In fact, some translators understand Wisdom to be described in verse 22 as a child "conceived" by God, rather than as "created" (NRSV) by God.[6]

This idea of Wisdom as a part of God, yet somehow separately identifiable, is also taken up in several passages in the New

Testament, where Christ is spoken of as the Wisdom of God. In 1 Corinthians 1:24 the apostle Paul writes of "Christ the power of God and the wisdom of God," and in verse 30 he describes Christ Jesus as the one "who became for us wisdom from God." This same concept of Wisdom is also described, using a different vocabulary, in the opening verses of the Gospel of John:

> In the beginning was the Word, and the Word was with God, and the Word was God. He was in the beginning with God. All things came into being through him, and without him not one thing came into being. (John 1:1–3a)

Here in John it is the "Word" that is described as present in the beginning. The Word is with God and yet also is God, like Wisdom in Proverbs 8. The Word was present before anything was made, and is essential to bringing creation into existence, as is also Wisdom in Proverbs 8. In John's Gospel, the Word is Christ, just as for Paul Wisdom is Christ. When early church theologians sought to explain the relationship between Christ and God, they connected these New Testament texts about Word and Wisdom to each other and then to Proverbs 8:22–31.[7] Christ was God, but still was a separate being intimately connected to God. Christ the Wisdom of God was present "in the beginning" with God and continues to be present with God forever. If we understand Proverbs 31 as a metaphorical description of the benefits that come to human beings who relate themselves to Wisdom Woman, then it can also become a metaphorical description of the benefits of our relationship with Christ.

But the metaphor also involves marriage imagery, and in discussing Gomer in chapter 5, I suggested that we should be alert to potential dangers inherent in speaking of the church as the bride of Christ. When we take the biblical metaphor into the human realm, we face two dangers. First, the metaphor can be misused in ways that blame the wife for whatever goes wrong. Second it can be misused to suggest that a power differential between husband and wife (or between men and women generally) is required by the biblical analogy to Christ as the head of the church.

When we turn to Proverbs and the image of Wisdom Woman, the pattern of the marriage metaphor is reversed. In Hosea, the human community was represented as female, while the divine marriage partner was male. Here in Proverbs the human community is represented as male, while the marriage partner who gives every good gift is represented as female. As Wisdom (Hebrew *Hokmah;* Greek *Sophia*) is identified with Christ, the image invites us to move beyond the language of the New Testament and to imagine the church also as the husband of Christ rather than only as the bride of Christ.

This image is of course so jarring that it is difficult even to get one's mind around it. Yet it may offer a way ahead in the face of the problems associated with Hosea's metaphor. Our sense that the alternative metaphor of the church as the husband of Christ is strange and incongruous should help us to realize that the traditional, more familiar, metaphor should also not be accepted as literal. If we can claim both metaphors, the metaphor of a male God with a female human community as bride, and the metaphor of a female God with a male human community as husband, then the partiality of each may be able to correct the other, and we may deepen and enrich our understanding of the God who is beyond all human imagining.

### Questions for Personal Reflection or Group Study

1. What has been your own experience of hearing Proverbs 31 in church or family settings?
2. Did you identify with some of the women in the imaginary Bible study group more than with others? Explore the reasons for your response.
3. In what ways (if any) can this text be a source of encouragement in your life? In what ways (if any) do you find it unhelpful?
4. Although no women in biblical narrative seem to match the description of the good wife very closely, perhaps you have known a woman for whom this text is appropriate. If so, describe her. Do you feel called to emulate her? Why or why not?

5. In most communities today there are some families in which the father has primary home and child-care responsibilities while the wife works outside the home. How do you think these men would react to this poem?
6. The idea that the text might be about Wisdom Woman instead of an ordinary woman is a big step from traditional readings. How do you react to this possibility?
7. The possibility of a metaphor for the relation between God and humanity in which the people are portrayed as husband and God as wife may be new to you. Keeping in mind that this does *not* mean that God is female (from earliest times Christian theologians have insisted that God is not male or female, but beyond human gender), how might this idea help you to reach a deeper understanding of God?

## Notes

1. Madipoane Masenya, "Proverbs 31:10–31 in a South African Context: A Reading for the Liberation of African (Northern Sotho) Women," in *Reading the Bible as Women: Perspectives from Africa, Asia, and Latin America* (ed. Phyllis Bird; Atlanta: Scholars Press, 1997).
2. For summary and evaluation of this comparison, see Alice Bach, "The Pleasure of Her Text," in *The Pleasure of Her Text: Feminist Readings of Biblical and Historical Texts* (ed. Alice Bach; Philadelphia: Trinity Press International, 1990), 30–31.
3. See "The Wisdom Woman" in Kathleen M. O'Connor, *The Wisdom Literature* (Wilmington, Del.: M. Glazier, 1988), 59–85. See also Christine Yoder, *Wisdom as a Woman of Substance: A Socioeconomic Reading of Proverbs 1–9 and 31:10–31* (New York: Walter de Gruyter, 2001).
4. O'Connor, *The Wisdom Literature*, 77, 79.
5. Ibid., 62–63.
6. Roland Murphy, "Wisdom in the OT," *Anchor Bible Dictionary* (ed. David Noel Freedman et al.; New York: Doubleday, 1992), 6:927; Claudia Camp, *Wisdom and the Feminine in the Book of Proverbs* (Decatur, Ga.: Almond Press, 1985), 84, 306.
7. See Kathleen McVey, "In Praise of Sophia: The Witness of Tradition," in *Women, Gender, and Christian Community* (ed. Jane Dempsey Douglass and James F. Kay; Louisville, Ky.: Westminster John Knox Press, 1997), 34–45.

# Suggestions for Further Reading

Bird, Phyllis, ed. *Reading the Bible as Women: Perspectives from Africa, Asia, and Latin America*. Atlanta: Scholars Press, 1997.

Brock, Rita Nakashima, and Susan Brooks Thistlethwaite. *Casting Stones: Prostitution and Liberation in Asia and the United States*. Minneapolis: Fortress Press, 1996.

Dalaker, Joseph. *Poverty in the United States: 2000*. U.S. Census Bureau, Current Population Reports, Series P60–214. U.S. Government Printing Office, Washington, D.C., 2001. <http://www.census.gov/prod/2001pubs/p60–214.pdf>

Darr, Katheryn Pfisterer. *Far More Precious than Jewels: Perspectives on Biblical Women*. Louisville, Ky.: Westminster John Knox Press, 1991.

Douglass, Jane Dempsey, and James F. Kay, eds. *Women, Gender, and Christian Community*. Louisville, Ky.: Westminster John Knox Press, 1997.

Exum, J. Cheryl. *Plotted, Shot, and Painted: Cultural Representations of Biblical Women*. Sheffield: Sheffield Academic Press, 1996.

Fewell, Danna Nolan, and David Miller Gunn. *Compromising Redemption: Relating Characters in the Book of Ruth*. Louisville, Ky.: Westminster John Knox Press, 1990.

Gallares, Judette A. *Images of Faith: Spirituality of Women in the Old Testament*. Maryknoll, N.Y.: Orbis Books, 1992.

Geitz, Elizabeth, et al., eds. *Women's Uncommon Prayers: Our Lives Revealed, Nurtured, Celebrated*. Harrisburg, Pa.: Morehouse Publishing, 2000.

Hess, Carol Lakey. *Caretakers of Our Common House: Women's Development in Communities of Faith*. Nashville: Abingdon Press, 1997.

Lee, Oo Chung, et al., eds. *Women of Courage: Asian Women Reading the Bible*. Seoul, Korea: Asian Women's Resource Centre for Culture and Theology, 1992.

Lorde, Audre. *Sister Outsider: Essays and Speeches*. Trumansburg, N.Y.: Crossing Press, 1984.

135

National Economic Council Interagency Working Group on Social Security. "Women and Retirement Security." Released on October 27, 1998. <http://www.ssa.gov/policy/pubs/sswomen.pdf>

Newsom, Carol A., and Sharon H. Ringe, eds. *Women's Bible Commentary: Expanded Edition with Apocrypha.* Louisville, Ky.: Westminster John Knox Press, 1998.

O'Connor, Kathleen M. *The Wisdom Literature.* Wilmington, Del.: M. Glazier, 1988.

Pobee, John S., and Bärbel von Wartenberg-Potter, eds. *New Eyes for Reading: Biblical and Theological Reflections by Women from the Third World.* Geneva: World Council of Churches, 1986.

Russell, Letty M., ed. *Feminist Interpretation of the Bible.* Philadelphia: Westminster Press, 1985.

Sakenfeld, Katharine Doob. "Feminist Biblical Interpretation." *Theology Today* 46, no. 2 (1989): 154–68. <http://theologytoday.ptsem.edu/search/index-browse.htm>

———. *Ruth.* Interpretation Commentary Series. Louisville, Ky.: Westminster John Knox Press, 1999.

Trible, Phyllis. *God and the Rhetoric of Sexuality.* Philadelphia: Fortress Press, 1978.

———. *Texts of Terror: Literary-Feminist Readings of Biblical Narratives.* Philadelphia: Fortress Press, 1984.

Van Wijk-Bos, Johanna W. H. *Reimagining God: The Case for Scriptural Diversity.* Louisville, Ky.: Westminster John Knox Press, 1995.

Walker, Alice. *In Search of Our Mothers' Gardens.* San Diego: Harcourt Brace Jovanovich, 1983.

Weems, Renita J. *Just a Sister Away: A Womanist Vision of Women's Relationships in the Bible.* San Diego: LuraMedia, 1988.

———. *Battered Love: Marriage, Sex, and Violence in the Hebrew Prophets.* Minneapolis: Fortress Press, 1995.

Williams, Delores S. *Sisters in the Wilderness: The Challenge of Womanist God-Talk.* Maryknoll, N.Y.: Orbis Books, 1993.

*Women: Challenges to the Year 2000.* New York: United Nations, 1991.